CW00829299

THE
MODERN
MUSE

How to Create the Ravishing Life
You've Always Wanted

GISELLE KOY

Copyright © 2010 Giselle Koy
All rights reserved.

ISBN: 1456300385
ISBN-13: 9781456300388

For Daniel and Lana

FORTUNA BOOKS

With special thanks to my muses:

Shayen (Dreamsicle), Rick, Sasha White, Ashtar, Gioconda,
Gwynn Griffith, Isha, Jennifer Hill Robenalt, Joe Marshalla,
Dimitrius, Nina Mercedes Ramirez, Alice Carrington Foultz,
Ann Elizabeth Santos, Juliet, Bijoy Goswami, Vlada,
Ariel Gruber, Babaji, Megan Pierce, Kelly Gish Daigle,
Lonn Friend, Baron & Lawren Sunderland.

"*The Modern Muse is medicine for the soul. As a musician, sometimes you need to be reminded that inspiration can come from the wildest places. Giselle has helped me to know myself and where my music can go. This book is for anyone who wants to be real no matter what.*"

— Rick Dufay, Musician/Composer/Former Aerosmith Guitarist

"*Very insightful and inspiring. Giselle highlights new doorways and paths to enlightenment with fun examples and insight. Another map on the highway to higher consciousness and understanding.*"

— Omar Rosales, Author of *Elemental Shaman/Director of Heaven in Exile*

TABLE OF CONTENTS

INTRODUCTION

F orever, there have been two approaches to God. One believes that you have to go through someone or something else to connect with the divine. The other believes that you can commune directly with the divine at any time and for any reason.

The first of these two belief systems is best represented by affiliation with a church, religion, spiritual leader or guru offering a connection with the divine.

The second is best represented by any practice that in someway reflects the ancient Gnostics, who were not only advocates but also proponents of connecting directly with the divine in an individual and direct way.

These two approaches have been "The Ways" for thousands of years. Yet, now we have evolved beyond these ways.

Now, there is a New Paradigm alive on this planet. This new paradigm extends to all of us the opportunity to directly connect with whatever divine we believe exists without any training being required and without having to go through any intermediary source.

In all actuality that bond has always been available to all of us, and has been waiting patiently for ever so long for us to reach up and grasp it. Having grown tired of waiting, waiting, waiting, this connection, all on its own, has decided to bridge the gap between itself and us, enabling the direct connection our souls have always sought.

As a result, individuals began fleeing from the over-whelming confines and restrictions of religion and churches, beginning in the 1990s. In fact, the United States seems to be going through an unprecedented change in religious practices. Large numbers of American adults are disaffiliating themselves from Christianity and from other organized religions. "The proportion of the [American] population that can be classified as Christian has declined from 86% in 1990 to 77% in 2001," states an American Religious Identification Survey (ARIS) Study. In addition, according to the 2004 *National Opinion Research Center*'s General Social Survey, "the number of Protestants soon will slip below 50 percent of the nation's population." In response, even the staunchest denominations have all suddenly become more flexible, choosing to overcome their rigidity rather than perish, especially in the areas of morality. However, the number of fundamentalists in Christianity and other traditional religions remains on the rise. These groups channel their religion into extremely rigid rules and actions.

Many progressive people have become disillusioned with their gurus as well as finding that those that "disempower" them do a tremendous disservice. The Tibetan Lama, Lama Palden, sees the guru in the Tibetan Buddhist tradition as someone who has *a profound love and trust of the Dharma, and whose path it is to empower the student to individuate.* A good teacher, she said, is a "stepping stone or doorway towards realization that the guru is within."

In the new paradigm we have entered, in which the planetary energies continue to shift to a higher vibration, more and more people are waking up to the truth within. According to a survey by pollster Lou Harris in 2008, 97% of the American people say that they believe in God. So while most of us believe that God exists, we are not necessarily called to join specific religions, churches or other spiritual organizations. The ways we refer to God can be Great Spirit, The Source, The Universe, The Higher Power, The Presence or any name that works for the individual. This is what the new paradigm is all about: higher consciousness on a massive scale. Buddhist Zen Master Thich Nhat Hanh has said, "we are here to awaken from the illusion of our separateness." Higher consciousness is the "one" of all of us, living our lives as divine beings and perceiving the world around us as a reflection of this divinity. It is new territory we have entered, the Aquarian Age where Planet Earth is assisting us to connect to God directly.

According to a recent article by Hal Blacker in *Enlighten-Next Magazine*,

> Poet and author Andrew Harvey has become another respected leader for many spiritual seekers. Having left his guru Mother Meera, whom he had only recently proclaimed to be the avatar who would save the world, he now has this to say about spiritual teachers and the nature of enlightenment: 'I think that the true spiritual guide admits that he or she is still in process, that they are always aware of their own shadow and of the limitations of their upbringing, their cultural conditioning, their particular religious views. The true spiritual guide never claims to be unified with the divine.' Although the author of a trilogy of books about remarkable gurus—including Mother Meera, his deceased Lama Thuksey Rinpoche and Jalaluddin Rumi—Harvey now sees himself as the bringer of a 'new paradigm' that seems to reject the possibility of unqualified wholeness and purity, and therefore also the possibility of a realized teacher who can fully embody these quali-

ties. (*Source: EnlightenNext Magazine*; www.enlighten-next. org)

The world doesn't need another religion or guru in this new paradigm that does not take us to ourselves. In fact, our "new teacher" may not even be a teacher at all. "It is possible that the next Buddha will not take the form of an individual. The next Buddha may take the form of a community, a community practicing understanding and loving kindness, a community practicing mindful living. And the practice can be carried out as a group, as a city, as a nation. . . For a future to be possible, our enlightenment must be collective." (Thich Nhat Hanh)

ABOUT MUSES

CHAPTER 1

WE ARE THE NEW GURUS

I have spent most of my adult life looking for the one person who could show me a way to enlightenment—the path to God. I spent six years in close proximity to a spiritual master in a mystery school in the progressive capital city of Austin, Texas. A mystery school is a private, invitation-only group of people dedicated to studying the same spiritual directives under the leadership of one guru. The gatherings are conducted in secret to ensure that students are not harshly judged or misunderstood by peers, friends, family or the outside world. Many of the teachings are unconventional and sometimes controversial. After longing all my life for a teacher or master who could facilitate a deep awakening in me, I found one. Or so I thought.

There were one-hundred and twenty others of like mind who wanted to be shown the way to enlightenment as well.

Our spiritual community was an ashram without walls and kept secret from the outside world. This was not easy but necessary for the intense immersion into the life of a devotee as created by the master. It was also necessary to avoid the judgment, opinions and criticisms of society.

The core teaching of the school was that awakening happens by being fully immersed in life. We were allowed to exist in the world, but were to avoid buying into the mechanisms and "group think" of the world. We were encouraged to use daily life as our dharma. In fact, we used all of our human experiences to wake up.

I had many transcendent experiences and learned how to ascend through sacred breath work and many hours of meditation. We learned to see the unchecked ego, the comparing mind, the never-ending wheel of distraction, and the seeds of samskara (desire) that could be awakened at any moment and take us away from our true path. We learned that we were not our minds. We learned about selfless service, love, keeping company with those of like mind and devotion to meditation. It was a traditional mystery school in many regards yet ultimately it failed me. In the end, the guru was exposed for not being that which he said he was. He fell from grace into the powers of sexual desire, a fact which he hid from many of us. He was having a very human experience even though he claimed to be beyond it. What was the final result?

The only guru is truth.

And that truth must be experienced within. Someone can point the way up the mountain, but climbing is an individual experience.

What else did I learn? That we are all having a human experience and that no one in a human body is immune from this. No one is immune from falling in love, having his or her heart broken, feeling frustrated, angry or lonely. Having embraced my humanity, I'm not even "looking" for enlightenment anymore. I don't even know what enlightenment means exactly. I used to see it as a goal I could reach in which suffering no longer existed. I thought enlightenment was a divinely blissful state, no matter what was happening around me. But this is not true. Even the gurus and the teachers and the leaders are living the human experience at some level. We can live in very high states of consciousness and still have emotions. The difference is that maybe we don't react and instead just witness these emotions or release them for the energy that they are.

Do we need help finding the guru within? Absolutely. There are many teachers out there who brilliantly direct us to our own truth.

"It is not for me or anyone else to tell you who and what to follow. Your heart will guide you if only you will truly and deeply honor the truth of your own heart. Any genuine teacher and path would tell you the same. And if they do not, then you have cause to doubt their genuineness and purity," says Brother ChiSing of the Awakening Heart Organization.

Even still, everyone, including spiritual teachers and leaders, need reminders and inspiration from time to time of who we really are. We are all here having this human experience and it wouldn't be a human experience without allowing ourselves to feel the full range of human emotions. This can mean having the freedom to absolutely enjoy any experience and it can also mean the wisdom to not act on a desire but just witness it for what it is. And it means having great compassion for the self. Once you know that you are a spiritual being having this human experience, you can let yourself off the hook, so to speak. You can have a depth of understanding for yourself that gives you an immensely compassionate viewpoint.

How are we finding the guru within? Through whatever touches, inspires or connects us to that which is our divine nature. There is a wide open field from which to choose. There are as many ways to connect as there are individuals. Some connect through nature, through scripture study, study of the masters and their texts, through yoga, through channels, through meditation, through creativity, through guides, through each other: the list is endless.

And then there are books. There are more and more books written all the time on this very subject; that of self-improvement and transformation. The self-help industry is an $11 billion dollar per year industry. Self-help books are those that are written to improve people's economic, emotional, physical, and intellectual foundations and can have a significant psychological and spiritual influence. I am focusing on those books based on spiritual improvement or books about transformation. People are looking for ways to transform themselves and their lives. That is why it is called "self" help because people want to help themselves. People are spiritually hungry and since there are so many ways to reach God and our divine selves, there is room for many voices to be heard on this subject. Is that a bad thing? No. We may have to hear it fifty different times, in fifty different ways and by fifty different voices until one day, something clicks. We are all looking for our unique blueprint, our unique path, our unique contributions and our unique gifts to share. We don't know exactly what will reach out and touch us at what time and cause the tiny shift or major transformation we have been waiting for.

The guru is being replaced by the inner guru and the new spiritual teacher is the one who helps us feel better about being human, about how we choose to live our lives. The new spiritual teacher helps us learn about loving ourselves, about loving what is and about our greatest potential. The new teacher is the one who teaches that we are all just divine beings having this human experience and the way to divinity is by embracing this experience and all of its flavors.

The new teacher is directly connecting us to God, not to him or her.

The new teacher proposes that desire is in fact a divine path and that feeling good is our birthright. We shouldn't have to work so hard to find our divinity as it is usually right under our noses. But we have been taught that we have to "work" for anything good and that usually sacrifice and suffering are part of reaching our goals. So we need permission—permission to feel good. We need permission to go for what we really want and permission to know that our desires are divine information.

And why shouldn't there be joy along the way, as well as pleasure, delight, play, sensuality and excitement? Right now in my life, I want to go to the bookstore and get something juicy so I don't have to work so hard. I want chocolate covered sushi; the protein and the dessert together, jet fuel with a cherry on top. I want my new spiritual meal to be packed with potency, fun, inspiration, and a little danger; something I can relate to and something that interests me. I have read many of the great spiritual teachings and loved them as each one has rocked my world. There is always a time and a place in someone's life to deepen one's knowledge and faith through the study of spiritual teachings and scriptures. My journey has lasted most of my life.

There are texts that transmit "living truth." These are texts that are eternally alive with a high vibration of truth. Some of my favorites are Eckart Tolles's *The Power of Now*, Yogananda's *Autobiography of a Yogi*, the ecstatic poetry of Rumi and anything by Osho.

So why am I not reaching for these classic texts at night? As crazy as it sounds, it feels like I am done reading for a while. Also, these books feel "spiritual." Being "spiritual" is like a cat trying to be a cat. He is already a cat. Why would he try and become something that he already is? That's silly. Yet we as spiritual beings want to become more spiritual. Actually it should be the other way around. We as spiritual beings should want to become more human. That is what this book is about— giving ourselves permission to become more human and to fully embrace our divinity through our humanity. Otherwise, why are we here in a physical body?

I hear people all the time saying that they feel unfulfilled and want to become more "spiritual." So they do what we are all trained to do: look outside the self and one's own experiences. The truth is that it is just ourselves we are out of touch with. Our teachers need to help us connect to God by ourselves. Anything other than that, in which we give up our power to another person, is a betrayal of self. This book is all about returning to the innocent, intuitive, heart-desire driven, child-like approach to life.

I want a new take on living a ravishingly lush and pro-found life that embraces not "trying" to be spiritual and not looking or behaving like I am "spiritual." Spirituality will never go out of style because our true nature transcends any kind of style. But the way we approach it as we grow and transform changes flavors from time to time. Sometimes we are devout and reverent and sometimes we are craving the colorful, lusty world. It just seems like the times right now are about reaching the sacred through the human buffet. Maybe sexy is the new spiritual?

What I am most excited about and where my fire burns brightly these days is in the "playing."

- Playing in this new flavor of highly creative energy that is available to us now in the new paradigm which is lightening fast, fueled by intuition and inspiration.
- Playing and co-creating, which is just playing with others with an intention to create.
- Finding the play in everything.

For example, in writing this book, when I make it "work" and struggle with research or anything other than playing, enjoying and having fun, it becomes something I probably would not want to read and something I'm probably not supposed to be writing.

I love this ravishing new energy that feels too good to be true, but really it is too good not to be true. I call this new flavor of consciousness the Modern Muse and She is here for divine inspiration in every area of our lives.

CHAPTER 2

DIMENSIONAL SLIDING: BRIDGING THE MYTHIC AND THE MODERN

There was a time in human history when people were familiar with the principles of the "unseen" universe in daily life. Before organized religion, humans had a sense of the magical and turned toward nature and the cosmos to understand our place in the universe and how life worked. Now, the influence of intuition—our sixth and most powerful sense— is all but forgotten. From the time we are born, we are systematically taught that our physical reality is what we should rely on for information, truth and even happiness. Now, we believe more in the pages of a magazine than the truth in our hearts and the knowing we were born with. Happily, we can return to this state not through years of hard meditation and therapy, but with a decision and a commitment to see things as they really are. In doing this, we are cultivating the emotional, psychological and spiritual intelligence to see situations from every possible perspective. What may have started out as one story emerges as many.

One night, my 14 year-old daughter "borrowed" my car. The police soon caught her and I immediately went to pick her up. As I was driving, I was engulfed in a complex psychic stew of shock, fear, relief, anger, disappointment, confusion and more. I collapsed into a parent who was horrified at what could have happened and ecstatic that my child was safe and did not injure herself or anyone else. I was also a parent who was thunderously angry at such a breach of trust and such a serious and life-threatening act of rebellion. Going a step further, however, I could also see it as a cry for attention and the innocent act of a child who simply wanted to ride through the hills, feel free and listen to Sly and the Family Stone blaring through the speakers with her girlfriend. For my part, it is a conscious choice to see all sides, take them in and choose how to react. In this situation, I found the strength to express my love and empathy for this extraordinary young woman I am privileged to call my daughter. But with hugs and kisses also came the decision to assert appropriate boundaries and a loss of privileges. Why? Isn't life to be enjoyed and embraced? Why are there rules if we are supposed to live a spontaneous and free existence? In this case, my daughter's choice created emotional havoc and fear in the family. In the new paradigm, our desires can uplift and inspire or create chaos and that is the difference between ego desire and heart desire.

There is another way of seeing things from every possible perspective, which can begin in a deep state of meditation. What began as simply relaxing and clearing my mind while enjoying the sunset at Zilker Park suddenly transformed into a sensation of melting into the "soup" that makes up this physical reality. I had closed my eyes to deepen this feeling, and upon opening them, I had no point of reference. I was blending into the scenery, the tree I could see, the young man and his daughter who were playing nearby, the dog, the air, the wind, and the totality of everything that was in my visual field. It was a transcendent moment of higher perspective, dissolving into love. It was grace that took me to that moment, nothing I did. I cannot be in that state at will, but it does visit on some auspicious moments.

When I have the opportunity to enjoy these high moments, I know that there are many realities happening in many dimensions simultaneously. Again, I could view that same scene: One day I was in Zilker Park and I enjoyed a beautiful sunset. I saw a man, his child and a dog. Period. What is the difference between the flat observation and the transcendent consciousness? I call it "Dimensional Sliding."

First, one must acknowledge that not only is there always a higher perspective, but that it is essential that our hearts and minds are open enough to receive the incredible information that comes from this perspective. And this perspective can be as simple as one look around.

I can turn and look at the person who is making my juice at the juice bar and see so much in that face. I can see an ancient being who has come here once again for his divine purpose. I can see the noble attributes of a disciple in the person sitting next to me in meditation. I can see the guy who walks into the coffee shop as a physical representation of Pan – the mythic companion of the nymphs with a penchant for mischief and who represents fertility and Spring. He appears in the flesh, showing up just like I asked and knew he would. I can see the tenderness of a Madonna in my daughter's face when she picks up our cat. I can see the wisdom of a sooth-sayer when my son offers his brilliantly innocent guidance to me. I can look up and see the moon, the same moon that mystics have been looking at for centuries. I can turn a corner in the magical city of Venice and see a Michelangelo returning home from a long night's work, exhausted and spent.

I can see myself in a traffic accident in Austin as some guidance to *slow my life down and be more present* because I wasn't listening to the other signs saying the same thing.

I can see my repeated failure at getting someone's attention as an indication that I am not supposed to get his or her attention. I can see my other failures as self-correcting measures here to guide me. I can see my attachment to how I look not as a judgment, but as the human desire for beauty, within and without. I can see my bad mood not as something I always create but the product of some energy that is not mine, but that has somehow attached itself to me.

I can see myself as a struggling ego that wants to be heard and seen and acknowledged or I can see a bright light just wanting to shine.

Nothing is ever as it appears in this line of work.

HOW DOES DIMENSIONAL SLIDING WORK?

Yellowstone National Park is famous for its many impressive geysers spraying water up in the air in a symphony of nature that delights and excites. The pressure from the ground causes it to shoot high into the air making a fountain that did not exist even moments before. Now, imagine that this is not water, but energy. Mother Earth is similarly providing a certain kind of pressure right now that is causing energy to spurt out in spiritual geysers across the globe. This energy is creative, sparkling and new. If you stand on top of one of these energetic spouts, you can be elevated to a new energy field, and an entirely different dimension. And these energetic geysers are never-ending, unlike the physical geysers that spurt and then retreat, the energetic geysers that exist in a world beyond the physical dimension are continuously flowing upward. They provide a never-ending flow of energy. As you stand atop one of these geysers and in this new dimension, you are being supported by the grounding energy of Mother Earth, which is assisting you in connecting to the celestial realm. "As above, so below."

This process is called alignment. And when we are in alignment, we are afforded a viewpoint along any section of that scale: from the earthly to the heavenly.

HOW DO WE STAND ON THE GEYSER?

Well that is the million-dollar question. We all want to be on that geyser all the time, even though I'm not really sure we're supposed to be there 100% of the time. Otherwise, we wouldn't have all the flavors of this dimension or the contrast which creates the flavors. If you are like me, you are there sometimes and but not always. In fact, I am still capable of plummeting to the depths of misery. The one thing I know to do when I am not on the geyser is to check my Vibrational Diet.

Your Vibrational Diet consists of everything you are exposed to on a moment to moment basis including: food, people, sound, weather, internal thoughts and relationships. It is basically a quick survey of the toxic -vs- harmonious levels in your life. It is a matter of taking an honest assessment of what is contributing joy, ease and happiness to your life as compared to what is causing suffering. Another important factor is to just allow and love what is. If I am in a place that feels terrible, so be it. I know it will pass just like the weather.

But how you perceive yourself is more than the mood or the state of being. It is a moment-to-moment choice. It is very powerful to state that you are choosing the highest perspective constantly. A good mantra for this practice is:

Today, I make my life sacred again.

Once we return to that geyser, that supporting, joyful, bubbly place of existence, remember to enjoy!

CHAPTER 3

MY MUSE STORY

I have meditated daily for ten years. I have studied yoga and have become a yoga teacher. My longing for something "more" than life as we know it has been a guiding force in my life. I wanted to rise above the hardships of this human existence. Like most of us, pain is a significant motivator. At times, I have suffered from depression, anxiety, loneliness and terrible heartbreak. One of my biggest heartbreaks was when my boyfriend committed suicide at the age of eighteen. We were in love and it happened on the night of my sister's wedding. My beautiful blond, curly-haired boyfriend took his own life at the cusp of becoming a man. This was followed many years later by another heartbreak when my older sister was murdered by her boyfriend. Her life was taken at age thirty-six by a brutal kick from her boyfriend. The circumstances of both these events were so tragic that it is still unbearable to recount even to this day.

These events created a pain I will never completely be free from although tremendous healing has occurred. I think we reach a level of pain and either grow or begin to die. We have the potential to die a spiritual death by avoiding life through drugs, isolation, boredom, bitterness, addiction, or simply ignoring that small, still voice within that is trying to wake us up to a joyful reality. I started down a treacherous road but somehow, through grace, woke up to life again. I went on to college and thrived in a creative environment. I always maintained my deep yearning to find more, be more and experience more. I just knew that life as I knew it was not all there was.

My saving grace has always been creativity. I studied ballet since the second grade as well as painting, drawing, writing poetry, designing clothes—anything where creativity reigns. It has been the tool that connects me to a meditative alpha state, which instantly takes me beyond the mundane and into the magical.

I am attracted to the revolutionary, the rebellious and life with an eye toward the extreme. I did everything to the extreme, including life within my marriage. I had it all. I was married to a successful man and had two beautiful children. At one point I had everything I was told a woman could possibly want. I had the dream. But like countless women of every culture, so many of us want more. We long to connect with that deep, authentic part of ourselves that becomes latent and neglected. When I realized my life was not working, I was too embarrassed to come clean. I confided in my mother that I was not happy, and she replied,

"What did you expect in marriage, to be happy?"

Well, yes, as a matter of fact I did expect to be happy. I cultivated this idea that it was time to reclaim myself, and at the same time we were planning a move to Austin, Texas. Then, after the move, a most fortuitous thing started to happen. I began meeting my "people." There were artists, dancers, writers, musicians and an opportunity to reconnect to my creative life in a way I had not done in my marriage.

In addition to the promising creative landscape that Austin offered, I met people who meditated and spent their lives pursuing spiritual knowledge. I was very attracted to this newfound family of conscious individuals who made healing, transformation, meditation and enlightenment major life priorities. They just seemed to glow. They were healthy and centered, but there was something about this new group of friends that I could not put my finger on. They all had something I wanted. They were unique in so many ways. For example, they all seemed to offer "selfless service" to others. Not for money, but just for the gift of it.

I remember one person who helped a paraplegic man everyday, bathing and taking care of his body. He did it for absolutely no pay. This really touched me and was so far removed from the life I had been living.

They also took extraordinary care of their bodies. No alcohol or sugar entered their diets, and they ate organic foods. They seemed to have a different language as well. They talked about the ego and the mind. They gazed into each other's eyes for minutes at a time. They talked about consciousness and "waking up" and "dissolving" in love. They seemed to live on a different wavelength than I had ever experienced before. And they lived with "less." I had been living a lifestyle that was all about more and more as we strived to amass wealth. These new friends had very humble jobs like preparing healthy foods, teaching yoga, Tai Chi and dance. They seemed to live a life richer than most of the rich people I knew.

They gazed into my eyes and held the gaze. A chasm began to form in my life between my new friends and my old friends. I was in two worlds that didn't quite meet. It was as if there was a jumping off point for me and I had to choose which path to take in life. It felt that big. My soul called me to choose my new way and let my marriage run its course. I didn't want to try and fix it anymore. I was worn out with the agonizing, the talking and the trying. And I wanted to begin a new life.

After the divorce I committed to a life-changing spiritual practice. I studied yoga and became a yoga teacher. But I deeply yearned for my own teacher. I asked the universe from my heart to send me one. I wanted to have a guide who could take me where I had never been and could not go myself. The closer I got to all of my new friends, the more I began to realize that there was a teacher in their midst. As time went by, the existence of this teacher was slowly revealed to me, and it was by invitation only that one could meet him. This process took years. I was eventually allowed to write to this teacher, and so of course I sent poetry expressing my desire to meet him.

This was a modern day Mystery School, in the tradition of the ancients, something unknown to me. And, of course, I wanted to be a part of it. Eventually I was invited to meet the master. Thus began six years of studying, meditating and being a part of a spiritual community, known as the Buddha Field. It was a complete immersion into a spiritual life, yet we were an ashram without walls. I still lived at home and took care of my children, but I spent many hours a week in gatherings. I also met privately with the master who worked with cleansing wounds that needed healing.

One of the gifts I got out of this experience was the ability to ascend into previously untouched higher realms of consciousness. We spent hours a day in meditation, both alone and in groups. Techniques were revealed to us using breath and focus, which took us to other states. We were given "shakti" frequently, which was like receiving a divine current of love, which ran like nectar through our bodies. We learned about distraction from truth and how the ego was designed to sabotage our lives. We were taught that to escape the ego, one could simply choose to ascend. In other words, you could use meditation as a tool to just "get out of your mind" or your ego.

For me, releasing the ego was and continues to be a frustrating, confusing and sometimes painful experience. In modern life, we are often confronted with interpersonal conflicts that test our ability to transcend. For example, what would you do if your best friend slept with your boyfriend? The teachings of this master told us to, "get out of your mind and go meditate." For most of us, this is unfathomable. But I was determined to master meditation and reign in my ego no matter what it took. I wanted to be able to jump over all the bumps in the road. I wanted to transcend the pain of all the negative human emotions including jealousy, envy, possessiveness and greed.

I was operating under the belief that this is why all the spiritual masters seemed so calm and unfettered by life. Problems were like water on a duck's back. The essence was that through ascension one could become liberated from emotional pain and suffering.

What I did not know at the time was that no one in a body escapes the human experience. I also did not know that I was becoming good at leaving my body. The ascending breath practice is all about taking the energy from the base of the spine and sending it up through the spinal column and out through the third eye. It was the practice of energetically leaving the body as a preparation for death and higher realms. At some point I grew attached to this state. It was like being on the mountain top and looking down. It felt lighter, freer and I noticed I was not getting caught up in the messy stickiness of life. I was living above all that. If there is such a thing as a spiritual snob, I was one.

This six year period of serving a spiritual master was one of the most intense bonding, growing and mind-blowing (literally) experiences in my life. In fact, I have written a book called "White Hot & Quiet" to describe this incredibly intense journey. Eventually, this spiritual community dissolved because of scandal surrounding the master. "Nothing is ever as it appears," one of his first teachings, became one of his last as well. He was exposed for not being who he represented himself to be. I did learn most of all, once again, truth is the only guru.

It took years for many of us in the Buddha Field to regain our bearings and re-incorporate back into civilian life, so to speak. Personally, I felt that I was done with seeking the outer guru in my life and began to focus on the journey of the inner guru. This was a major turning point in my life.

However, one day while reading a magazine, I was instantly drawn to a tiny photo of a woman's face. It was an article on a spiritual teacher in South America. My first reaction was, "oh no, I am done with gurus." And I truly was. Yet somehow I was drawn to her. I didn't know if we were destined to be friends or what the pull was but it was strong enough for me to consider going.

So after gathering the necessary resources, that is exactly what I did. Off I went. After an initial few days in Buenos Aires I went to her spiritual retreat. When I met her, we had an instant connection. I was part of a large group where she was giving "darshan," a sanskrit word meaning the sharing of truth. Afterwards she came up to me and said, "Hello."

In our next encounter I was in the group listening to her darshan again. She pointed me out and startled me by saying, "GET BACK IN YOUR BODY!"

Obviously this jarred me because I was in a very blissful state in that moment. Wasn't this the whole point? To be in a blissful state?

Later when I had a chance to speak to her she explained that she could see me leaving for another dimension. I knew she was right, but I was confused. Why was that a bad thing? It had taken me years to be able to do that.

She then explained that enlightenment is not through leaving the body but through really being in the body. This was contradictory to everything I had been taught. But I was open to learning. I knew I was there for a reason. A big part of her teaching was:

To be fully divine, you must be fully human.

Then I watched her. Soon, we did become friends and I spent time seeing how she lived. She was not about being "spiritual" at all. She was an enlightened, beautiful, modern, busy woman who ran a large spiritual retreat center and had a normal life. She didn't want people to worship her. I was very inspired by her and so relieved to be out of "following a guru." I knew that I could never follow one again because I was on my own divine path. And so began my life devoted to the full human experience. Fully engaged means just that, you are ALL in. It is accepting the fact that we are all having a unique human experience.

What does that mean exactly? It means that we are here to experience it all, not just the things we want to experience: to see that every experience is just that, an experience. We have learned to categorize and judge our experiences as either good or bad, but they are all just experiences. We are the ones that put a plus sign or a minus sign in front of them.

The human *experience* puts us all on a level playing field. It also helps us to have compassion for ourselves in knowing that not one human being is immune from feeling the full spectrum of emotions. Just as no one is immune from getting hurt, no one is immune from falling in love either. I love this fact. No one is immune to love. This fact is comforting to me because it puts every human being on a ....human level. We are all designed to experience the incredible gifts of human emotion. Let them be our guide. All we have to do is feel them: not fix them or ignore them, but let them pass for the energy that they are.

CHAPTER 4

WHAT IS A MODERN MUSE?

There is a way to live your life beyond what you may think. There is a way to go beyond the ordinary to find the ease, leave the desert and go into the ocean. There is a way to step out of misery and find love so deep, so grand, so huge and so wonderful that you are living life beyond your wildest imagination. The spirit of the ancient Muse has returned to take you on the journey that will challenge everything you once knew about how to live your life. There is a way to connect to this consciousness through fun, enjoyment and the spirit of a child awakening to the world for the first time. There is a way to enter this Joy-Based-Economy and to know that all we are here to do is to love, enjoy life and be in joy.

And what is this joy-based economy? In the new paradigm, the new currency is happiness and feeling good. This feeling is a substance that has real value, and is in widespread circulation. It is what we work for and how we want to get compensated. But mostly it is what we value. We know the value of monetary currency and the lifestyle it can provide but what we really want this currency to provide ultimately is enjoyment and deep satisfaction.

Joy is our natural state. And the beautiful thing is that it is what we are supposed to be reaching for. It will become easier to make a choice based on joy. In the past I would make a choice that involved suffering if I thought it would bring me gain, but now I think twice and reach for the joy choice more and more.

And how do we access this place? It is through the full human experience. It is from living a fully engaged life, truly accepting whatever is happening at any given moment. While positive thinking certainly has its place, we cannot deny the scope of human emotions that are a sign of who we really are. Our emotions are gifts to direct us, guide us, and help us grow, expand. Exploring the world of Muse energy is about feeling completely O.K. with where you are and who you are. If we have no measuring stick or internal judge there is no comparison. The comparison is from duality. So what if you are hungry, have lost your job, or have been abused? There is always a higher perspective to consider and it is endless. Marcus Aurelius said, "The universe is transformation."

So in the moment we may not know why this person has no money or food, but there is a plan in place and a message being delivered. There is a higher perspective beyond what all of us can see. And it is unending. Above all, there is trust that the journey can take us to remarkable places if we stop asking, "Why?" and start asking "What is next beyond my wildest imagination?"

I am not here to save the world and thank God for that. I can honestly say I have no desire to save the world. That sounds like too much work and impossible. But I do get excited about helping others to save their own personal worlds, including finding their life purpose. A Muse helps people to identify what they desire to do. Imagine a world where everyone understood how his or her skills, passions and talents could help humanity and transform our lives. All I know is that if I do exactly what I want to do, I will inspire other people somehow. It is that easy.

So why are people questioning their place in the greater scheme of things now more than ever before? Because there is a gift coming from the universe that reveals a highly sparkling creative energy designed to assist us in living the joyous and spontaneous lives we were meant to live. For the first time in human history, there is an entirely new flavor of consciousness that is available to every human being on Earth. This constant, streaming energy is so delicious, juicy, fluid and lovely it completely challenges any idea we ever had about the possibilities of beauty and love in our lives. What began with the mythology of the Greeks – the introduction of muse consciousness and the intervention and support of the Gods and Goddesses – is now the foundation and the framework of a new creative golden age in this century.

I call this energy the Modern Muse.

The energy that defines the Modern Muse is ravaging and ravishing. It will have its way with you. This consciousness will take you and throw you down on the bed and mess your hair up and intoxicate you with inspiration. It will electrify you with a tingling sensation that will permeate your entire being. It is like Pan, the mythical bad boy: instinctual, raw, sexing up virgins at the watering hole, taking what he wants and devouring you. Once you have this ravishing lover, you are hooked. By the end of this encounter, you will experience the sweetness of satisfaction that comes only with knowing that the old ways will soon be transformed into a new way of life that speaks deeply to how human beings were meant to live. A metaphorical roll in the hay with Pan or Muse energy is irreverent, sexy and above all, life-changing.

So how do we begin to incorporate the mystery of ancient mythologies into our everyday existence? How do we meet Pan or bring the energy of the Modern Muse back? Even more importantly, how can human beings benefit from this knowledge and gain access to the universal consciousness which binds us together?

Desire.

It is through our plain, simple, red hot, lip-burning, spine-tingling desire that we begin to understand. It is that pure desire that comes directly from an open heart. Not ego desire, but instinctual desire. The desire you were born with and which brought you to this moment. Finding your true desire and acting on this powerful instinct may indeed be the real secret of the universe. Ultimately, our desires are our secret roadmap to who we really are and what our role is in the larger universe.

Who we truly desire to love is whom we are supposed to love. What we truly want to do is what we are supposed to be doing in life. That which we desire to create is what we are supposed to be creating.

It really is as simple as that. Imagine if you could live your life, spending every second just being in touch with feeling your desire and what you want most. How would your life change? "Imagination is just a preview for coming attractions."- Albert Einstein

Most of us have this popular perception about muses that most likely originated in elementary school when we began to learn about Greek mythology. I remember marveling at how glamorous, exotic and powerful these magical beings seemed. But even though we were taught that the mythological realm was superstitious, primitive and not real, I felt there was something deeply authentic about what we were learning. On the physical front, maybe we couldn't prove the existence of magical beings in elaborate councils in the sky. But the creative energy and thought behind this mythology was tapping into a critical mass consciousness that we are only now beginning to experience again. That's right. It's back.

For centuries we've grown up in a society that values science and objectivity, which is great for things like medical and technological advancements. But in the areas of self-awareness, new thought, transformation and spirituality, the return to mythology as a gateway to understanding consciousness is making its debut all over again. To understand ourselves as the co-creators of our future, let's look at our heroic past.

The nine Muses were the love children of Zeus and Mnemosyne, the goddess of memory. According to Hesiod's Theogony (seventh-century BC), they made love for nine consecutive nights and the results were Calliope, Ourania, Euterpe, Thaleia, Erato, Kleio, Polyhymnia, Terpsikhore, Melpomene. Each of these lovely celestial ladies had a particular focus for the creative soul. People believed they were the spirits that fueled the creative process for poets and artists and, of course, musicians. We think of muses as the basis for music, museums and amusement—methods or facilities that deliver enjoyment, inspiration, creativity and joy.

Isn't it appropriate that the mother of the nine muses was related to memory? Creativity in art, in business and in how one leads a unique life is all about remembering who you really are and what you really desire in this lifetime. The power of the muse is helping those who struggle with reconnecting with our truest selves. This is not just for the artist. This is for the art of living.

Most of what we know about muses was captured in the poems and songs of their time and passed through the generations in a powerful and intimate oral tradition. But as in all oral traditions, there are many versions of how the muses came to be.

In another story according to Pausanias in the later second century, Aiode, (song or voice), Melete (practice or occasion) and Mneme (memory) were the three original muses. In Delphi three Muses are also acknowledged by the names of three chords of the lyre, an ancient stringed instrument: Nētē, Mesē, and Hypatē. They were later called Cēphisso, Apollonis, and Borysthenis, which historians say identify them as the daughters of Apollo.

In understanding the roles and origins of muse mythology, we get some insight into how to access and act upon the creative spirit. Living a deliberate and consciously creative existence requires that we commit to understanding new ways of thinking, new ideas and even new processes. Diving deeper into muse roles may help us shake off those cobwebs and begin practicing the power of asking for support and guidance from unknown sources. So what are their roles?

Calliope: She is the eldest Muse and the leader of all muses. In Greek, kallos means "beauty" and "ops" means voice. She is the muse of epic poetry and elegance and is typically shown with a writing tablet.

Ourania: Her name translates to "heaven" and her areas of concentration are astrology and astronomy. She often wears a beautiful crown of stars and carries a celestial globe.

Euterpe: "Eu" means "good or true" and "terpein" means "to please." She is the beloved muse of poetry and music and is often in possession of a lyre and a crown of flowers.

Thaleia: Her name is the combination of "young" and "blooming." Her territory includes comedy and the idyllic. She can be seen with a funny mask and a shepherd's staff.

Erato: In Greek, "erastos" means "to love." This beautiful muse inspires people to write lyric and love poetry and to mime or mimic. Like Euterpe, she also carries the ancient, stringed lyre.

Kleio: She is the muse of history and her name in Greek means "to celebrate, praise or tell." When you see Kleio, she is most likely identified with a book or a scroll.

Polyhymnia: She is the muse of sacred poetry and oratory and is depicted with a pensive expression. Sometimes she wears a crown of pearls or flowers. Her name has origins in Greek, Latin and Middle English and roughly means "many hymns."

Terpsikhore: She is the muse of dancers and dramatic chorus and her name may mean, "dance loving" and "to delight." She also carries a lyre and wears a flower garland.

Melpomene: She is the songstress, the singer of the group. The Greek translation of "Melpein" is "to sing." Her identifying characteristics are wearing a helmet or tragic mask, and carrying a knife.

So it is the spirit of the ancient muse which is back: fresh, new and even better than before that is helping to transform this planet. This new energy is a gift from the Earth itself for all of us to slide and play around in! So along with this new playground we find ourselves in, comes new ways to play as well. All we have to do is learn how to play again. In life. In love. In work.

AWAKENING THE MUSE WITHIN

CHAPTER 5

STEWING IN OUR "ISNESS"

Years ago, I saw a movie starring Sharon Stone called *The Muse*. She plays the role of a successful creative muse to a variety of very grateful Hollywood directors and writers. She lives as she pleases, shamelessly pursuing beauty and never apologizing for her lifestyle or her process, which is unpredictable. Her method comes from the realm of inspiration which has no timeframe or standard operating procedure. She never felt as if she had to explain herself. She knew who she was. She was a muse.

When I was looking for my next job, nothing I could think of seemed to satisfy or excite me. There was really nothing out there that seemed to fit. All the jobs (and there have been many) served their purpose at the time.

So when I saw this movie, my heart leapt. Not only could I do that, I had been living the life of the muse for many, many years. Of course, there was an aspect of self-talk that went something like, "well that is just a movie, you can't do that. That would just be too easy and too much fun and too natural and everyone would snicker and say you were a big ego or worse... crazy." So I just parked the idea in my mind as something I was very attracted to.

I never forgot about it, but I just wasn't ready to fiercely go for what made my heart sing. Until one day, years later, it hit me. I am not looking for a job, I am looking for my "role" in life. And guess what? It looks a lot like that movie! I was already "musing" people in my life before I knew this was my role. When I accepted this as my role, extraordinarily even more people began to magically appear. This happens when you are completely aligned with your role and doing the work you would do for free, with passion and serving the highest good. Everyone has a dharma or a soul purpose in this life. I feel so privileged to have found mine because it is what I love to do. It's a great job because it's not a job. When I made the shift from job consciousness to role consciousness everything immediately changed for the better.

Life becomes ravishing when you fall in love with the full human experience and fully engage in life. You may fall in love, get hurt, express emotions, experiment, love fearlessly, risk, go out on a limb, and not care what other people think.

There is a way of being that makes us more potent.
It is stewing in our "isness."

Being more potent means being a more authentic, stronger version of yourself. Stewing in our "isness" beautifully amplifies our unique vibration. It puts out our scent in much stronger, more tangible ways. It releases our individuality.

When I stew in my "isness" I slightly withdraw from the daily drama of life and make my inner world more important than my outer world. I go inside and listen and feel more deeply. I become the espresso version of myself. This brings me closer to my authentic self. I can hear guidance better and I can play more. I become more mischievous because I am not taking the world so seriously. I am a little bit more free to be exactly who I am. When this happens, I live more purposefully. When I am more purposeful, I am more aligned. And when I am in alignment, I am in the flow. This way of living also brings rewards to everyone around me. And being in the divine flow is the birthright of every human being.

CHAPTER 6

IS THERE ANY MORE CAKE?

There is freedom in feeling your feelings fully; everything from throwing a temper tantrum to having supreme appreciation for your life. You get to experience all of it! The idea is to feel fully but become more of a witness to this experience. It comes back to the "if you observe it, it changes" law of physics. Once you observe or witness the emotion you are having, just the observation alone shifts the emotion.

Say you are overcome with jealousy. You could quit fighting the jealousy and just admit to yourself, "I am so jealous right now." The observation changes the behavior just like atoms change when we observe them.

It's important to express your emotions because you're not living your full human experience if you're not feeling.

We've all heard "You have to feel to heal." So many people are afraid to feel. It is fear that keeps us from feeling, but our nature is to feel. Our nature is to have all types of weather pass through; sunny days and storms. There is nothing to do during a thunderstorm but let it pass. It always does. When you know this, even in the middle of a storm, there is an acceptance of "what is" and loving "what is" is even better. And if you're not feeling it, that means that some form of fear or disconnection is holding your emotions back.

The human experience is all about not being afraid to feel. It is seeing emotions as energy that just needs to flow, meaning felt and expressed, not held inside. Unfortunately many of us are taught that emotions should be suppressed, like boys who are taught not to cry or that vulnerability is a sign of weakness. What an awakening it was for me when I learned that my strength was my vulnerability.

Have you ever looked at "your story" as just "a story?" Here's mine:

I grew up in a dysfunctional household where affection was suppressed and rarely expressed. It was a rigid authoritarian environment and I turned rebellious and escaped through art and other means. I was taught that the power came from the person in charge instead of coming from inside. This made me a ripe candidate to become involved in a spiritual community with a master who had all the answers. Eventually I disconnected from this community as the leader turned out to be something other than what I thought. I still learned many things, the most important thing being that the guru is on the inside.

Everyone has a tale of woe. Rarely does anyone have an idyllic childhood and rarely does anyone escape the facts of life such as birth trauma, adolescence, heartbreak, tragedy, death, addiction, financial drama, health crisis, etc. And yet we all think that our story is precious.

Your story is unique, but it is also just a story, no more shameful or tragic or amazingly wonderful than anyone's story. It is just the journey that has brought you to "now." When I realized my story was just a story, I was able to let go of much of the shame surrounding my life history.

How we navigate emotions is very different. We all have a degree to which we will allow ourselves to fully experience an emotion. Usually there is a pain or discomfort threshold that limits us, except for children because they have no filters. They fully experience their feelings because they haven't been conditioned to self-judge, control, hide, displace or avoid feeling. They just are feeling beings.

I have many tricks that I use to avoid feeling. I notice when I want to avoid and what my particular method of escape is. I make a joke to avoid an uncomfortable situation,

I go and work out to avoid feeling angry, I go have a frozen yogurt when I am lonely, and the list goes on. It is nothing too terrible, but there is still avoidance. Lately I have invited the full feeling of emotions to be present.

First, I am practicing naming the emotion. Instead of just "feeling like shit," I pause and check in to see what I am really feeling. I rewind a bit and think, "Oh yeah, I'm feeling anxiety about that conversation I just had."

As crazy as this sounds, I was so disconnected from my feelings I would actually ask people how I was supposed to be feeling in a given situation. I would watch movies and make mental notes about what feelings were appropriate. Recently I found a list of feelings based on the book by Marshall B Rosenberg, Ph.D., titled "Non violent Communication."

After identifying the feeling, I try to just experience. And just by observing the situation, once again, I change it. Spiritual texts refer to this as "becoming the witness." I feel the tension in my body and the cellular agitation that accompanies anxiety.

And then, I have to let it go. And by letting it go, I do not mean meditating my way out of it, I mean expressing it. I may say to myself, "Wow, I am really anxious about this situation." Sometimes I punch the bag at the gym. Sometimes I call a friend and just ask if I can vent. I make sure that they know they don't have to fix or save or help me. I want them just to listen. Then, I feel better. My friend Dr. Joe Marshalla calls it, E-Motion. Energy in Motion.

Emotions are just energies that need to be released.

There have been several lengthy experiments done with people who express emotions and those that don't. The bottom line is that it is a scientific fact that not expressing emotions makes you sick.

According to the research staff at EmotionalProcessing. org.uk:

Emotional expression can have a variety of effects on social interactions, psychological well-being and physical health. A popular, yet controversial belief held by cultures and clinicians alike is that failure to express emotion is psychologically and physically harmful. Numerous empirical studies have demonstrated both mental and physical health benefits associated with emotional expression, as well as negative psychological effects, which are associated with inhibited expression. (Pennebaker, 1995, University of Texas at Austin)

The process of consciously inhibiting emotional expressions while being emotionally aroused, referred to as expressive suppression, has been shown to be disruptive to communication. Butler and her colleagues (2003) discovered that expressive suppression can reduce rapport and inhibit relationship formation between individuals. More intriguingly so, their research suggests such suppression produced a unique physiological stress for the individual engaged in conversation with the suppressor. For example, "an increase in these individuals' blood pressures was observed."

There is a fourth aspect to the benefits of feeling your emotions fully. And that is in order to allow yourself to fully feel everything, you have to love yourself. Shame is one of the biggest causes of pain on a deep level and many times there is shame attached to experiencing and expressing emotion. Shame is not guilt. Guilt can be a guide from our moral compass to keep ourselves in check. On the other hand, shame comes from our emotional imprinting as children with the basic belief that there is something wrong with us. Shame can be sexual, emotional, mental, physical or spiritual. It can also be collective such as a whole culture believing that they are less than another culture. Shame has many layers and we usually aren't even aware of how much it frames our experiences.

A simple example is the male conditioning in our society. In our culture, it is a sign of weakness to cry; many hold a belief that there is something wrong with them if they feel and express even a basic emotion such as sadness or grief.

I know in order to feel, I have to love myself. If I am experiencing jealousy or envy, there is a certain amount of shame and judgment that I am experiencing these lower emotions. But when I am consciously loving myself, I will allow myself to feel those emotions with no judgment. I will accept them as part of my human emotion.

Is there a state beyond the emotions?

I always thought that once I mastered my emotions or evolved enough, I would be free from irritation, impatience, the comparing mind, the envious mind, the ambitious mind and all the things that cause suffering. But my experience has been quite the opposite.

I notice that I can still have little tolerance for lower vibrating energy. I can be more impatient than ever in traffic, or when I have a conversation with someone who feels unconscious or stuck in negative thoughts and behaviors. To me, the telltale sign is simply whether or not I feel energized, empowered, nurtured, understood or light when I am with someone. If I don't feel any of those things, I have less tolerance. I just want to leave right then and there. Sometimes I do after I try and politely remove myself from the situation. I still yell in traffic. I want my ice cream when I want it. I'm not sure if I am just learning how to fully feel everything or if my vibration has shifted to one of just not being able to stand being in lower vibrating energy.

There is the story of the Tibetan lama who comes to visit the U.S. after many years. He is a very respected and renowned teacher who has not spoken in a while and the spiritual world is waiting with baited breath to hear his first words. So he comes to the packed lecture hall and takes the podium. The crowd becomes still as he leans in to the microphone. Finally, he will share his great wisdom. The first words out of his mouth: "Is there any more cake?"

I love this story. I love this lama. He loves himself so much that he is not afraid to fully feel his emotions. He has no filter, no shame and no performance anxiety. He is like a child, so deep in the present moment with no judgment. Some people in the crowd might have felt a little disappointed. And I'm sure there were others who celebrated this man in his glorious authenticity.

There is such freedom in being ourselves. Authenticity is a supreme state of being. Imagine the freedom to totally love ourselves so much that we can be ourselves in every moment. No shame, no guilt, no judgment. Just "isness."

Once we accept ourselves truly for who we are, we view humankind differently. When I don't judge myself for being who I truly am, I appreciate others for their uniqueness. It is what makes this dimension so colorful.

I catch myself when there is judgment and let it go. Yesterday I was in the grocery store in Sedona, Arizona. I saw an older woman, maybe in her sixties wearing a very low cut tank top. She had long gray hair teased up and had on high heels and cut-off shorts. There was a flash of that old paradigm voice in my head that wanted to judge, but only for a second. I really appreciated her for dressing with freedom, being herself, not caring what others thought and showing her femininity. I was inspired by her. Freedom is sexy. Fully embracing our condition is accepting that we are all having the human experience.

To get in touch with your feelings, name them, feel them, and express them is liberating.

CHAPTER 7

THE INNER MUSE

Traditionally, a muse is something or someone outside ourselves—a force or spirit of nature that moves us to create and become exceptional. But musing is also a flavor of consciousness which people can use with each other or alone at any moment. Musing is the alignment of three things: *Creativity, Desire and Purpose* (CDP). That is the trifecta. When those three things line up in your life, you know where you're going and what you're doing. You're not searching for that elusive experience to define your happiness anymore. You are in alignment.

Desire comes from the heart and is one of our most effective tools given to us from birth to help us find our way. But for many, desire is a "bad" thing rooted in attachment, superficiality or darkness. We are taught that to not

desire anything is to achieve a state of spiritual enlightenment where we do not need or want anything outside ourselves to feel whole. We are taught to control and suppress
desire. But in doing this, we do not look deeply enough into
the role and purpose of desire in our lives.

> *Desire is a divine clue, which can direct us to*
> *what the universal consciousness wants from us.*

To ignore this principle leaves us sadly in the dark about
how to live the best life possible.

You can make your life better by incorporating the qualities of the muse into your everyday life, infusing them with
authenticity, present awareness, creativity and your heart's
desire. When you're making those qualities your priorities,
and incorporating them into your consciousness, you will
observe a profound change in your life.

The key to experiencing the core of muse consciousness is allowing yourself to find what creates a sense of fun,
excitement and relaxation in your life.

If we were standing in your physical shoes, that
would be our dominant quest: Entertaining Yourself,
pleasing Yourself, connecting with Yourself, being
Yourself, enjoying Yourself, loving Yourself. Some

say, "Well, Abraham you teach selfishness. And we say, yes we do, yes we do, yes we do, because unless you are selfish enough to reach for that connection, you don't have anything to give anyone, anyway. And when you are selfish enough to make that connection – you have an enormous gift that you give everywhere you are. – *Abraham (Jerry and Esther Hicks)*

Certainly this idea is different for everyone, but wanting to feel good, enjoying and relaxing is a great way to create space for receiving information and gifts from the universe. This energetic shift in attitude instantly changes your vibration. When you relax, your vibration shifts into one of trusting. If I am not relaxed it's because I am not trusting. I am not trusting that I am going to get there in time, that I'm doing a good enough job, that I know enough or that good things are going to work out. Not relaxing is not trusting.

When you relax it's because you know it's all coming.

In this state, you're sitting back, you know that what's going to happen is going to be good. You are secure with where things are and where things are going, even if there is no evidence. Then relaxation and trust create space for the creativity, for the fun. We need that space in our heads. We need a certain a amount of free mental real estate in order to expand.

If we want to lose weight, it helps to relax. It is a known fact that cortisol levels (the relaxation response) are related to weight loss. Trusting creates relaxation. But what do we trust? We trust in the goodness of the universe. We trust that everything is in perfect order and happening at the perfect time. Trusting is knowing that all is perfect right now. All is well. So the question is, how can we relax more, have more fun, feel better and trust in all the good things coming to us?

The answer is different for everyone. Overworked. Overcommitted. Overextended. Most Americans struggle with an epic lack of time. But we can always poke holes in the schedule and make more space. There is always room for more space, for more relaxation, and for more enjoyment.

Trusting is knowing that everything is in divine perfection. I made a sign for my altar yesterday for the month of September. It says, "Sit back, relax, know that everything is coming at the perfect time and in the perfect way and there is nothing to do other than relax and enjoy things a little more." It's not an affirmation or positive thinking. It is a "relaxing" into the great love and really knowing it in every cell of your being.

Say you're writing a book. What if you already knew it's a bestseller? How would that affect your writing? You're probably going to be a lot more relaxed.

What if you lived your life knowing that your perfect partner was on his way to you?

What if you totally and truly knew that everything you're reaching for is reaching for you and it is simply a matter of that critical lineup of matching vibration. It's all right there.

What if you knew that the universe wants only the very best things for you and is busy making it all happen, beyond your wildest imagination?

What if you really knew that there is no doom and gloom, and had no fear whatsoever?

What if you really knew that in every part of your body, mind, heart and soul? How would you look, feel and speak differently?

What if you quit watching the news for a while, since it's the same news we've been hearing for thousands of years, unplugged from mass thought and plugged into your true self?

What if during the economic recession you knew that all is perfect and there is nothing to fear?

What if you knew there is no evil, that it is only misalignment?

What if my teenage daughter knew that her desire to express herself was actually the juiciest elixir of her life and not something to be afraid of?

This is how we create our world. The universe wants us to be joyful. The universe is good.

What you are reaching for is reaching for you.

THE TRIFECTA: CDP

(CREATIVITY, DESIRE, PURPOSE)

*If people actually understood that what you want to
do is what your are supposed to do, the world would
change because that is the truth.*

Creativity

Every single person has a specific job to do to contribute to consciousness. It may be as simple as smiling at the gatekeeper every morning. That act alone may have a tremendous reverberation, as in the Butterfly Effect. There's no judgment as to the scale of the act. There's no micro-macro view to acts of kindness. There is no difference between a small act of kindness and a grand scale act of kindness. They all vibrate to the universe at the same rate. An act of Mother Teresa and petting a kitten have the same vibration of love.

If you are one of those who believes that they have no special gifts or talents, it may be because you are waiting to discover it. The truth is you are most likely already expressing this gift because it is what you do naturally. What do you do for free? What do others value in you? Is it service oriented? Our gifts come in many flavors from serving to creating to facilitating to leading.

Desire

When we desire something, this is a clue to our life's purpose.

This may be the most popular subject right now for self help books: finding your life purpose through passion. But guess what? I do not believe you can say it enough times or enough ways. I remember when I was with my spiritual master he would repeat himself over and over again with the same teachings, but say them a little differently each time. Finally after years of hearing the truth or the wisdom again and again, it would one day take hold, it would sink in. I would hear it for the first time after hearing it for hundreds of time.

In fact, I think the fact that so many people are writing about this means that there are many people who want to hear it. I also think that there is plenty of room for all of the different voices. What appeals to one reader may not appeal to another. There is a need for all the flavors and diversity of messaging.

One of my favorite quotes on this subject is from Joseph Campbell who came out with the message to "follow your bliss." That was quite a profound statement at the time. Following your bliss means to follow your passion. And he is so right.

How to Find Your True Desire

Some things are too good not to be true. You've heard the expression "too good to be true." What is the opposite of that, when things are so good, you can't believe it? Well, just as some things are too good to be true, some things are so simple we just can't trust them. Important things aren't supposed to be simple and easy, we expect them to be complicated and difficult.

MYTH BUSTERS

Myth 1 It's too good to be true.

Myth 2 It can't be that simple.

Myth 3 Important decisions must be made carefully. The pros and cons have to be considered. Decisions take time and analysis. Also we need to poll all our friends. Or we need to ask everyone we know, or consult a psychic.

What if we trusted ourselves enough to know exactly what to do at exactly the right moment? We have lost touch with the initial response, the raw instinct, the true impulse that comes from our heart and not from our minds. It is called the "heart mind" in the Buddhist tradition. It is amazingly accurate, innocent and 100% truthful, but it has somehow gotten buried underneath the layers of the mind. I have had times when I have lost access to this guidance. But when it's working, here's how simple it is to use:

THE HEART LEAPING EXCERCISE

When facing a decision, *your heart leaps or it doesn't.* It sounds thrilling or it doesn't. It excites you or it doesn't. You desire it or you don't. If the answer is "maybe a little," that is a no. That's how easy it is.

Let's try it on some basic questions:

1. Am I in love or not with someone? No, because either you are or you aren't.
2. What should I do with my career, take Job A or Job B? Actually, neither one sounds good, but it's better than the job I have now. Should I take it? No.
3. You're lonely. Paul asks you out. You don't have anything better to do. Besides, your mother always said, "you never know who his friends may be." Do you go? No, your heart leaps or it doesn't.

Living your life true to your heart sends a message to the universe that you are not settling. Not only are you not settling, you are raising your standards.

Why do we go to the movies? TO FEEL. It's impossible for me to watch a romantic comedy and not have at least one moment when they get together when my heart leaps and I say to myself, "That's what I want!" The desire is stirred. THAT, right there. THAT is the potent medicine we are looking for. THAT sends a very powerful vibration out into the world like a heat seeking missile, trying to find a vibrational match. That's how it works. THAT flavor of vibration is sent into orbit on a quest to find the exact same flavor vibration to connect with.

Finding Your Edge

Many of my clients tell me that they have "lost their edge." The "edge" is a feeling you get when you are going for a desire. It is when you are going for something that is going to make you feel better. The stronger the desire, the better the anticipated feeling and the more edge you bring to everything you do. It is reckless abandon brought to an ordinary action fueled by a strong desire. All the more reason to stay in touch with those sacred desires.

The Birds and the Bees

I have a tape recording of Osho speaking from his ashram garden in Puna, India. He gives a beautiful talk about the nature of desire which I couldn't begin to quote, but which had a profound effect on me. In all fairness and respect to him and his grand teachings, I can only write about the impressions it left on me. In fact, I was given a picture of the primal energy of the universe which has stuck with me ever since. What follows is my interpretation of his inspiring talk.

There is nothing in the universe that is not about sex. Attraction is the fuel behind all energy. It is the same with the birds and the bees as it is with the atoms. It is the same with universes in the cosmos. It is all based on the vibration of attraction. This is the most basic, most primal, most essential movement of all energy. There is nothing not in this flow.

In this model, desire informs us of this flow, this natural way. Desire is the divine information, guiding us along.

Purpose

The Trifecta is the alignment of all your ingredients.

- What are you good at? What just comes naturally? (Your Talent, Gift or **Creativity**)

- What is your passion? What would you do for free? (Passion or **Desire**)
- What is serving a higher purpose? This is where you surrender to the divine will. It is the true meaning of "Thy will be done." (**Purpose**)

How Do You Arrive at Your Own CDP Trifecta?

1. List five things you are good at.
2. List five things that you love doing, have already been doing your whole life and would do for free anyway.
3. Ask yourself how this may serve a higher purpose. In what areas does my personal agenda of success serve something greater than myself?

CHAPTER 9

GROUNDING: GROWING A TAIL

When my spiritual teacher told me "You are not in your body," I wanted to know where exactly I was? I really don't know the answer to this. I just know that in those spiritual states, I am not attached to the earth. It is as if I am floating above myself. This is one of the reasons it is so attractive because you don't have to be here. But what is the point if we cannot be here now? And just to set the record straight, it is not as if I am somewhere on an exciting adventure to another planet when I leave my body, I am just on a different frequency that is disconnected from the here and now. Remember dimensional sliding?

This created a whole new frontier to explore. What is grounding? How could I get grounded? What would that feel like? I remembered from yoga all the grounding exercises we practiced by rooting through our feet. So I began my experiment. I would sit in meditation and just begin to grow a tail. As if my spinal cord came out of my body and extended deep into the earth. Then I elaborated on this imagery. I made my tail a color and then I sent it down to the core of the earth. I passed through many ancient layers of sediment to finally reach the Earth's core. Then once I felt this root extending down, I anchored it. I grew an anchor on my tail and secured it to the core.

I practice this first thing upon waking in the morning and I find it to be a very powerful exercise that always brings up treasure. It is like tapping down into the collective well of creativity. Some image or idea or thought or message always bubbles up as a gift from Mother Earth. I keep a pen nearby to record these divine messages then usually act on them by writing or delivering a message to someone.

There are other ways of grounding and getting back in the body. Food can be grounding. I notice that when I fast I become unattached to the planet and lose myself. It is not a good feeling and it is usually accompanied by feelings of paranoia and insecurity. Mother Earth energy is nurturing and secure. At the first sign of not feeling these founda-tional roots, it is time to get grounded, once again.

I think of Mother Earth as a living being who is sits there with one thought; to support, love, and nurture us. To provide us with everything we need at all times. I used to think it is "the universe" providing everything we need but I have expanded this to see that the physical planet is helping now more than ever before. As above, so below.

Certain foods are more grounding than others. Raw foods tend to un-ground me while cooked warm foods seem to ground me. Sometimes I just want a large meal so I can literally feel heavier and more weighted on the planet.

Being in nature is grounding. Walking on dirt in bare feet is grounding. Going into my rose garden and just standing there is grounding as well as healing.

Another very powerful exercise is to see the earth as a single, huge organic creature that is constantly rising up to support our every move in this walk on earth. With every step we take, matter and energy are rising up under each foot to support and help us on our way. In fact so much matter is rising up around us, cities have been formed. Mountains have been formed from the earth energy rising up to meet us. Grounding helps us to literally connect to the earth.

CHAPTER 10

VIRTUES AND REFINEMENT

Virtues are good qualities. They have potency. They bring us into integrity with ourselves and with others. They vibrate on a high frequency and help us to stay in alignment with higher frequencies.

I feel virtues should be brought back on a large scale because whatever we observe we alter. So just by observing that we need more virtues we are assisting in bringing them back; just by making them conscious. Virtues refine our energy and everything is about refinement.

Higher consciousness IS refined energy.

Higher consciousness is remembering our connection to source. No doubt, it is our goal on an individual and planetary scale. Every aspect of our being now is about that.

What can people do to reconnect with the virtues? First of all, we can name them. There is an organization that promotes virtues known as Character First®. It lists fifty virtues and gives definitions.

CHARACTER FIRST®!

Alertness vs. Carelessness Being aware of what is taking place around me so I can have the right responses.

Attentiveness vs. Distraction Showing the worth of a person or task by giving my undivided concentration.

Availability vs. Self-Centeredness Making my own schedule and priorities secondary to the wishes of those I serve.

Benevolence vs. Selfishness Giving to others' basic needs without being motivated by personal reward.

Boldness vs. Fearfulness Confidence that what I have to say or do is true, right and just.

Cautioness vs. Rashness Knowing how important right timing is in accomplishing right actions.

Compassion vs. Indifference Investing whatever is necessary to heal the hurts of others.

Contentment vs. Covetousness Realizing that true happiness does not depend on material conditions.

Creativity vs. Underachievement Approaching a need, a task or an idea from a new perspective.

Decisiveness vs. Procrastination The ability to recognize key factors and finalize difficult decisions.

Deference vs. Rudeness Limiting my freedom so I do not offend the tastes of those around me.

Dependability vs. Inconsistency Fulfilling what I consented to do, even if it means unexpected sacrifice.

Determination vs. Faintheartedness Purposing to accomplish right goals at the right time, regardless of the opposition.

Diligence vs. Slothfulness Investing my time and energy to complete each task assigned to me.

Discernment vs. Shortsightedness Understanding the deeper reasons why things happen.

Discretion vs. Simplemindedness Recognizing and avoiding words, actions and attitudes that could bring undesirable consequences.

Endurance vs. Discouragement The inward strength to withstand stress and do my best.

Enthusiasm vs. Apathy Expressing joy in each task as I give it my best effort.

Faith vs. Presumption Confidence that actions rooted in good character will yield the best outcome, even when I cannot see how.

Flexibility vs. Resistance Willingness to change plans or ideas without getting upset.

Forgiveness vs. Rejection Clearing the record of those who have wronged me and not holding a grudge.

Generosity vs. Stinginess Carefully managing my resources so I can freely give to those in need.

Gentleness vs. Harshness Showing consideration and personal concern for others.

Gratefulness vs. Unthankfulness Letting others know by my words and actions how they have benefited my life.

Honor vs. Disrespect Respecting others because of the higher authorities they represent.

Hospitality vs. Loneliness Cheerfully sharing food, shelter and conversation to benefit others.

Humility vs. Arrogance Acknowledging that achievement results from the investment of others in my life.

Initiative vs. Idleness Recognizing and doing what needs to be done before I am asked to do it.

Joyfulness vs. Self-pity Maintaining a good attitude, even when faced with unpleasant conditions.

Justice vs. Corruption Taking personal responsibility to uphold what is pure, right and true.

Loyalty vs. Unfaithfulness using difficult times to demonstrate my commitment to those I serve.

Meekness vs. Anger Yielding my personal rights and expectations with a desire to serve.

Obedience vs. Willfulness Quickly and cheerfully carrying out the direction of those who are responsible for me.

Orderliness vs. Confusion Arranging myself and my surroundings to achieve greater efficiency.

Patience vs. Restlessness Accepting a difficult situation without giving a deadline to remove it.

Persuasiveness vs. Contentiousness Guiding vital truths around another's mental roadblocks.

Punctuality vs. Tardiness Showing esteem for others by doing the right thing at the right time.

Resourcefulness vs. Wastefulness Finding practical uses for that which others would overlook or discard.

Responsibility vs. Unreliability Knowing and doing what is expected of me.

Security vs. Anxiety Structuring my life around that which cannot be destroyed or taken away.

Self-Control vs. Self-Indulgence Rejecting wrong desires and doing what is right.

Sensitivity vs. Callousness Perceiving the true attitudes and emotions of those around me.

Sincerity vs. Hypocrisy Eagerness to do what is right with transparent motives.

Thoroughness vs. Incompleteness Knowing what factors will diminish the effectiveness of my work or words if neglected.

Thriftiness vs. Extravagance Allowing myself and others to spend only what is necessary.

Tolerance vs. prejudice Realizing that everyone is at varying levels of character development.

Truthfulness vs. deception Earning future trust by accurately reporting past facts.

Virtue vs. Impurity The moral excellence evident in my life as I consistently do what is right.

Wisdom vs. Foolishness Seeing and responding to life situations from a perspective that transcends my current circumstances.

© 2007 Copyright Character Training Institute. All rights reserved. Permission granted to reproduce in entirety for informational use only. Not for resale.

For more information, contact the Character Training Institute, www.characterfirst.com.

Hardly anyone teaches these, as if they've become old-fashioned and unpopular. However, I think they should be taught from a very early age. There is also a well-known book called "The Book of Virtues: A Treasury of Great Moral Stories," by Wililam J. Bennett.

So let's observe them and let them populate our consciousness. Once we know them, we can use the words in our daily language and let them infuse our lives. Right now

I'm inviting in the virtue of benevolence, which is kindness without any expectation of receiving credit.

5 Ways To Reconnect with Virtues
1. Learn the words.
2. Begin using the words.
3. Practice the words and see how many opportunities you have to embody that virtue. Focus on one at a time.
4. Recognize virtues in others.
5. Acknowledge them.

When my son does something that's full of integrity, I rave about it. His humility is so admirable, it totally changes my day. Call out extreme integrity. Let it be an inspiration for you. Call out the good when you see it. Call out the beauty in your life. Call out what you see that you appreciate. This is people musing each other.

Raving is complementing with passion. Add feeling to your compliments. This is a natural state of musing.

Speak with heart.

A lot of people are afraid to express because they have fear of articulation, which is another shame-based obstacle. But what needs to be articulated comes from the heart.

The words don't matter as much as the authenticity with which they are spoken. Speaking from the heart needs no articulation. It's the vibration of true communication that comes through. This expression changes people's day and it changes your day! Tell people how they are affecting you positively, not just negatively. This is the basis for intimacy.

See virtues in other people and rave about them.

An authentic exchange is what everyone wants, especially partners. Women who complain about men not being intimate really just want an authentic exchange. They want men to speak to them from their heart, from the world of feelings, which is typically a woman's natural habitat. They don't necessarily want a sophisticated Don Juan, nor someone who can recite poetry, but somebody who is willing to speak from his heart. Every single man is capable of speaking from the heart. Women are screaming for men to touch them with their words. "Relate to me on a heart level" is what women want to say. Sometimes it's easy for men to be passionate about what they're angry about. They could be passionate about what they are happy about as well. It's a big switch for people to be just as passionate about what we are happy about as what we are unhappy about. This way we all get in touch with our hearts.

CHAPTER 11

HOW THIS MUSE WORKS:

STAYING PREGNANT

Personally, I have set a vision for how I see THIS muse working. I am asking to work with those that have the most stroke, the most leverage, the most impact on the world. I am asking to work with the leaders, artists, musicians, thinkers, and agents of change in this new paradigm. I don't know who they are or how they will find me, but that is not really my job either. My only job is to stay in the flow. To stay in the state of synchronicity and magic: the realm of pure potential. I like to stay pregnant with ideas at every moment.

For example, I think of Eric Clapton and how I would like him to make a new album where his old album "Cream" left off. Maybe it would be called "Organic Cream." I would take 3 different musicians from three generations and mix them up for a new sound. Like the movie "It Might Get Loud" where Jimmy Page, Edge and Jack White combined forces to make some new kind of magic. I know for a fact there are many old lions of rock and roll lying about who should be paired with other generations and other genres. This is fertile ground with so much to explore.

I ask to work with all the stars whom I have not met that are ready to shine their brightest and help co-create this new community that is part of the new paradigm.

I ask to be that spark to whomever I come into contact with. My desire is to bring out the creator and artist within and help people to find that power for themselves. After all, you are the modern muse. You know who you are. If this book is in your hands or if somehow this has attracted your attention, you may have a calling to be a muse.

In this profession, magic is your new playground. Imagine you come from the angelic realm. Imagine that you no longer have free will and that the only thing that truly satisfies you is to serve others for the highest good of all. This doesn't mean you can't have fun; in fact, you are not in the muse energy when you are not having fun. Your life becomes your creation and how you live it is a direct expression of your freedom, doing what you love, and expressing your gift.

CHAPTER 12

WEAR WHAT YOU ARE

When I say that sexy may be the new spiritual, I am really talking about the divine feminine. It is goddess energy, which is about reflecting you inner radiance outwardly.

Sometimes I spend way too much time deciding what to wear. Laugh if you must. But as a sensitive person, I prefer to be in the right clothes or the right colors to match my vibration for the day. And that takes a while in the morning. But there is more to it than that. Our clothes are our adornment, our costumes, our stage wear. It is our packaging and our outer reflection of the inner. If you are connected to goddess energy, it is our royal robes, our shamanic cloaks, our courtly attire, our queenly gowns and/or our fierce armor. The connection includes, all those things and also it is an expression of creativity. It is self-expression. I really don't know who I want to be on any given day as far as presenting a face to the world. Sometimes I want to be Pan, sometimes the goddess. Sometimes the intergalactic princess. The possibilities are endless. I think everyone should be allowed to dress how they feel.

I see the world being more open to dressing freely. The Burning Man culture has created its own culture of dress: fantastical, magical, wicked, circus-like, clowny and haute—couture grand. I know that in the seduction community, "peacocking" is recommended for men. This is definitely breaking out of the old stereotype of how men should dress. It involves colors, jewelry, scarves and hats. I love seeing a man's hand with a big chunky ring on, maybe even with painted nails. I love tattoos. I love self-expression. It makes this dimension more colorful.

CHAPTER 13

CO-CREATION: THE THIRD THING

When I spend time in the coffee shops endlessly talking to people one-on-one something happens. Something was being created by the two of us being together. As a co-creator, I do not just give a person information or guidance, I put myself into it. I put my heart into it. We become intimate partners of a new creation. And when it happens, and it usually almost always does, it is magic. Honestly, I think it is the most fun I can possibly have on the planet. I guess you could say this job is truly my heart's desire.

I love bringing out the diamond in another. I love the act of co-creating. So what is the name for this job? There really isn't one, except for the word "musing." When this word popped into my head, it was like Zeus throwing a lightening bolt at me. It STRUCK me. In fact, in the world of ideas and creations, being struck by something is one of my favorite forms of INSPIRATION.

We hear the word co-creation a lot. It sounds like new paradigm lingo. What does it really mean? To me it means "the third thing." There is me and creativity and then there is you and creativity and then there is what happens when we come together. We create a third entity, that exists because of the unique combination of you and me. But it is not just about the end product, it is the act of creating together. This is where it gets really fun because an energy is created that is like an elixir. It feels like the spiral of a tornado. You can be swept away in it. Time flies and you don't even realize you're working on something. It just happens. You are so enmeshed that you become lost in the vortex of creation. It is other-worldly.

So here I was, in love with the word "muse." But wait, I could never call myself that. That is a word that other people call you. That is a name that is bestowed upon you, a title. Wouldn't it be egotistical to say I was a muse? That would be like a man calling himself "a renaissance man." Someone else should dub you that.

So I asked around. I polled my friends. They didn't really want to come out and say it but the opinions of those I most respect was that is wasn't something I could call myself. So I designed a website that talked about muses but never called myself one. I would let others dub me that. My clients could call me that. None of this was making my heart leap. The truth is that I KNOW I am a muse because I just KNOW. I know it deep down, I know that is what I am here to do and it is what I do naturally, whether I want to or not. So, I am just going to have to call it like it is, fearlessly and shamelessly. Part of finding our roles is just claiming them.

After I finally came to the realization that musing was my vocation, I became very ill. What started out as a kidney infection spread through me very quickly until I ended up in the emergency room after days of a high fever and severe dehydration. As I was lying in bed, still feverish, I called my healer friend to get "a higher perspective." He and his guides looked at me and he told me that I was close to death. "What?" I shrieked, although I did feel like I was losing all life force. I had been lying in bed for days now, feverish and sweating. It felt like a plague was upon me.

"Your cellular memory kicked in. You have been killed many times before for being a witch or a healer. Once you decided to hang your shingle up again, your cells began the dying process because that has been the story in the past. Now that you are doing what you came to do, you need to heal this within yourself. You know what to do. There is no turning back."

Surprisingly, I did know what to do. I hung up, closed my eyes and went back to visit those deaths from persecution. I saw before my mind's eyes a series of images. One was of my feet with chains around them, one was in the night being surrounded by hooded people, one was underwater, being pushed down. I went through each one and asked that the memories that my cells were holding onto be released. I spent a few minutes in this state, not much time, and then opened my eyes. It still took a day to recover but from that moment it felt like a train that was moving in one direction had been stopped and was reversing. A massive amount of energy was required to move the train in the opposite direction.

And the energy did move. I needed another day of rest but I was on the road to recovery. This may just sound like a story to you but it was a profound initiation and transformation for me of leaving the old imprinting behind and stepping into the new paradigm. The new paradigm is here to offer this accelerated healing to all of us: assistance beyond our wildest imaginations.

CHAPTER 14

NOTHING ADDED

When I first started musing, I felt like I had to "do" something. In other words, I was there to provide my services and needed to be in the space of healing, helping and doing. I was exhausted after a visit to one of my first clients, spending time with him in Arizona, giving all my energy to him and focusing every ounce of my creative being helping him on this next evolution. Several months later, upon my second visit to him I realized that I had dropped all my ideas of having to "do" anything. All I have to do is show up and be myself: be in trust and open to the universe. In fact, the more relaxed I am, the more creative I am...or anyone is for that matter. It was such a relief to know that all that was required of me was to show up. It takes great trust to know that whatever you need will show up exactly when you need it, however you need it.

There is an ease and a freedom that comes into life when you decide that you are enough, exactly as you are, in every moment. Nothing needs to be added. I once had a boyfriend who was physically beautiful: he had an elegant manner, a great presence, kindness and loads of personal magnetism. He had it all, yet he was always trying so hard by over dressing, over doing, over selling himself, just everything was a bit over done. I wanted to tell him that he was so perfect just as he was, that nothing needed to be added. Everything he TRIED to do just took away from all that he already was. Sometimes we do not need to prove anything because it's all there already.

We are all best just as we are.

CHAPTER 15

WE THINK WE ARE PEOPLE

Isn't enlightenment just highly advanced authenticity? Authenticity to the point of not even having a self to be? You are so authentic there is not even an idea of you that you are trying to uphold. You are free in every second to be exactly as you are, to the point of being who you truly are.

Dogs don't try to act like dogs. Hummingbirds don't try to act like hummingbirds, they just are. So why are we so different? We think we are people so we try to act like whatever our idea of people is. What if we were operating from the belief that we were divine spiritual beings who came to play and learn and experience joy? Then would we try and act like spiritual beings? No, we would just be ourselves, unabashedly. That is why we are here, to experience this human reality. . . to wake up in this body, while we are here in this sensual vintage dimension known as Planet Earth. To fully embody.

CHAPTER 16

THE OREO COOKIE

So being myself is the answer? Could that possibly be true? That I could just be exactly who I am in every second and never even try to impress, inform, fit expectations, blend in, or be normal? Wow, that could be fun. I would have to be pretty free to be like that. I would have to not care what other people think. I would have to live my life differently. I would have to rediscover what it is I actually like and dislike. I would have to really look at what I desire and don't desire. I wouldn't have to make any excuses for why I did what I did or why I do what I do. It's like eating the white part of the Oreo cookie. We don't have to eat the black cookie part if we don't want to. Wow, I want to live like that!

Who do you know living like that? Who inspires you to completely love yourself? Who loves themselves enough to be themselves, exactly as they are with no self-consciousness? When are you like that?

I find these self-actualized people irresistible. The lady working at the coffee shop who has no idea how bright and innocent her smile is while she serves coffee. The child without self-consciousness playing with his own hands and screaming when he wants his ice cream. My daughter when she is in the kitchen, lost in the sensual delights of inventing some new dish.

Me, using my desires as my path.

MUSE
TECHNOLOGY

CHAPTER 17

TUNING IN

Modern musing is based on Muse Technology. For me it starts with a vision. I may meet someone and get a glimpse of them in a more refined, polished state. It is not the same as seeing the potential in someone. That is based on a future projection, seeing them in a successful state once they reach some milestone. What I'm talking about is catching a glimpse behind the curtain. I get the feeling that "this person really has no idea about who they are."

Then there are the tools of intuition, mystery, magic, play, creativity and fun– all the good stuff that helps people get in touch with their creativity and their desires.

Message Delivery

Sometimes messages will come to me that need to be delivered. An example: Sandra Bullock opened up a restaurant in Austin. I went to see it and loved the experience but something wasn't right. It was the music. It just wasn't the right vibe. So I scribbled out a note and left it with the manager for her. She can certainly disregard the information, I was merely passing it along.

Serendipity

For business clients, it seems like I always pick up newspapers or a magazines that show me some pertinent information that he or she may need. For example, at the check out line, a headline from "THE ECONOMIST," a magazine I would never pick up, just jumped out at me. It was a news breaking story about an emerging market that my client was entering. It was the right piece of information at the right time. Or maybe I will see something random that I know he needs to know. If I was supposed to be doing research on what may help him in his emerging market, I could spend hours finding information but it may not be that single piece of information he needed at that time to make a big decision. That is muse technology at work.

Sparkling Intersection

I have been noticing a new level of synchronicity. It is when not only two auspicious things line up, but maybe three or four, all at the same time. Or maybe manifestation is occurring at such a rapid rate these days that it is accelerating these points of intersection. When these things happen, I always gasp at the magic. They are *aha moments* on a new scale of magnitude. I call these moments Sparkling Intersections. It is serendipity to the power of 10. And as we already know, there is no limit to how high things can go.

Finding Your Guidance

I have spent so much of my life trying to line up with guidance. I have always wanted to hear direct guidance in order to make decisions easier and better. I have always wanted to hear a voice in my head speaking, see an angel, see visions or have guides present themselves.

Guidance is different for every single person. There are those who feel information (clairsentient), those who hear (clairaudient) and those who see information (clairvoyant). For me, I have been hearing guidance my whole life, so much so that I think it is my own voice or my soul talking. I feel it is this way for many intuitive people. The "voice" of their guides or teachers or angels has been so constant that they think it is their own voice. Getting in touch with your direct, moment to moment guidance is what a large part of the self-help industry is all about. That magical hook-up of being in the flow: the trifecta of CDP in perfection.

So much of finding your guidance is about listening and noticing. If it is difficult to hear, feel, see or know what your guidance or intuition is, there is a simple way to connect, and that is to let the universe be your guide. It starts by simply noticing the signs around you: a song, a synchronicity, a recurring thought in your head, running into a person, having the urge to call or do something for no reason. Paying attention to these signs sends a signal to the universe that says, "hey I am listening and receptive."

Another way to follow your guidance, and one that is taught by Zen masters, is to "follow the path of least resistance." It sounds simple but how do you really apply it? Does it mean I can just lie in bed all morning and not get up because that is the path of least resistance? Does it mean to run from any conflict or difficulty that comes my way? Well, not exactly.

It is learning how to spot resistance first.

What does resistance feel like to you? To me, it feels like being out of sync with the flow, like nothing is happening, like frustration, or the inability to manifest or make anything happen. In many relationships, it felt like tremendous effort was required, or that I was doing all the pursuing, or that the connection was forced or that I was not being met.

Or that the other person just wasn't into it. Just like the movie "He's Just Not That Into You." So I became very clear about what resistance was looking like in my life. In fact, at the time, all I felt was resistance. Nothing was happening in my work life, there was no inspiration. I was lonely and I just couldn't seem to make a connection. It was a desert. Since I had nothing to lose, I decided to take the path of least resistance. I was going to make every decision based on whether or not I was being met by resistance. This was quite challenging because I have a strong will and was used to willing things to happen. I even took it a step further and decided that from that point on, it was clear what I would do.

Walk through open doors.

Not doors that were ajar, or halfway open, or slightly open, but only doors that were wide open. Bam, just flung open. It was then that I could clearly see how many doors I was trying to force open. So for someone who is a "doer" this is a whole new tactic to take. Sitting back and just noticing open doors? Well it took quite a bit of discipline and self-control. And then I had to just let everything crash around me. I just let go of all these things I was trying to make happen. I let my world just fall into a heap around me. Crash and burn.

I had to get honest about the relationships that weren't working and the ideas I had about what I was supposed to be doing. But I committed, and things slowly started to change. When I decided to only walk through open doors, things changed. It was as if I sent a message to the universe that I was no longer going to settle for things. I was no longer going to do things that were just kind of right. It is still a challenge, but enough change happened for me to realize that this policy does work for me and that this is one of the ways I am going to get my guidance.

What specifically changed for me was that I became clear about what I wanted to do. I wanted to be in direct alignment.

Finding your intuition

Intuition is how consciousness reaches us. It is through keen insight that just arrives without reason. I call it a "knowingness." It is different from inspiration in that inspiration is more of a theta burst. Some of us live through our intuition and let it guide us. Guidance is usually from a recognizable source such as a voice or a vision while intuition is just there, like instinct. It feels as if it is just built in.

Everyone has intuition.

Accessing it just becomes a matter of tuning into it. Sometimes we don't listen because it's not convenient or it's something we don't want to do. I know sometimes when I am attached to the way something should be and I ignore my intuition, nothing bad may happen, but it may take longer to get where I want to be. How many times has my intuition told me not to get involved with someone or not to enter into a certain business agreement but I ignored it? Plenty. Even if we have a little bit of anxiety, that is intuition telling us to at least be cautious and listen.

Dr. Joe Marshalla describes intuition as: "Knowing without explanation or reason. We've lost our connectedness to intuition because we have not been allowed to know something without first being able to explain it. Our whole life is spent explaining everything. And if we make a decision and can't explain it, then it is assumed that something must be wrong with us." He continues with saying, "How many times have you done what you knew you shouldn't have or not done what you knew you should have. In either scenario, you are met with disaster. Imagine never having to explain yourself to anyone. When one allows themselves to live through trusting their intuition in that natural state of awareness, then they are living a life filled with magic, purpose and passion."

The Voice of the Gut

Usually our heads (reason and logic) get in the way of hearing our own intuition. If we can leave the thinking out, we have a more direct channel. Even forming words to talk involves our minds. There is a sound you can make that short circuits the thinking brain and it is the "grunt." I know you are laughing right now, but it's true. So when I am having trouble listening or hearing my own intuition I ask a friend to ask me a series of questions. I will tell them what kind of questions to ask. Say I am trying to decide if I should go on a certain trip. Someone has extended a lovely invitation but I'm just not quite sure if I just want an escape or if I really need to be on this trip. So I will create a list of questions such as

~ How are you today?

My response. Uh.

~ How did you like your lunch?

Uhhoh.

~ What do you think about that person over there?

Uhhuuuuh.

~ How would it feel to win the lottery?

uhuhhhhh!

~How do you feel about traveling with Tony?

Uhhhhh.

~How do you feel about New Zealand?

Uhhhhh...

~ How do you feel about being in New Zealand with Tony?
Unnnnnn.

~ How do you feel about staying here and writing?
uh huh!

So just by the sound of your own voice, creating a gut-tural sound, you are listening to the voice of your own gut. And it's fun because you look and sound ridiculous which is an added bonus!

CHAPTER 18

TOOLS

Know thyself

I just got up to make a cup of tea and the message on my tea bag says "Without realizing who you are, happiness cannot come to you." The big perspective on this is that "self-realization" is just that: realizing who you are. There are so many levels to know oneself from the personality to the psychological to the total realization of your divinity. And there are tools to help with knowing each of these levels as well. If knowing oneself is loving oneself, I say we cannot know ourselves enough. Following are some of my favorite tools to facilitate self-knowledge.

Astrology

Of course, this is accessible to everyone and you can even get a reading in most daily newspapers across the country. I love Ron Breznsy's "Free Will Astrology". It is brilliantly written and always entertaining. The subject of astrology is far, wide and deep. Years of study are required to be a true astrologer.

Mayan Glyphs

This is information of a very different flavor. Using your exact moment of birth, you find the symbol which represents you. Then you can read about yourself from an ancient mayan cosmic point of view. The first time I read about me as Cauwac, I was dumb-founded because I felt like I was looking at my life since the orgin of time. When I give a reading with the Mayan Glyphs I always make it a ceremony because it should be done over hours. I like to burn some copal and have a celebration in reconnecting someone with this ancient knowledge about themselves.

Cards of Destiny

I was introduced to destiny cards while near the mouth of a volcano in Hawaii. A sage asked my birthday and then pulled out a sheet of paper. It had all the cards from a regular deck of playing cards listed and corresponding with every day of the year. He then explained how each suit had its own meaning.

- Hearts- relationship and love
- Spades- work as in putting your spade in the ground

- Diamonds- money and business
- Clubs- mental activity and creativity

Then beyond the basic theme for your life, or suit, there is a number. There are the royal cards; jack, queen and king. And then there are the numbers. I found this quite accurate and it is a very quick way to learn about someone.

I recommend *Cards of Destiny* by Sharon Jeffers and *The Power of Playing Cards: An Ancient System for Understanding Yourself, Your Destiny, & Your Relationships* by Geri Sullivan and Saffi Crawford (Paperback -Nov 30, 2004). One of my favorites is *Love Cards* by Robert Lee Camp. Books like these provide great information on relationships. You take the combined number of two people and it will give you a composite or what the blend of those two energies will create.

DNA Divination

Two fascinating systems I have found on the Internet are:

genekeys.net

geneticmatrix.com

These are advanced holistic systems based on the premise that every person's life purpose is hidden in their DNA. Highly complex and comprehensive, these programs combine branches of Vedic Astrology, Cartography, and the

I-Ching among others. This is for advanced divination as it takes time to study. It can take months to get familiar with the information, but I find it infinitely compelling in that it is a computer program (the new witches' cauldron) that shows us how we are genetically wired. It introduces a whole new model for viewing types of beings and offers strategies to hear your own guidance.

Oracles

Oracles are tools for divination or getting to the divinity of a situation. Many of them have been around for thousands of years and are used to see into the future and offer guidance. They get us in touch with divine information regarding the future, sort of like dousing for truth. It is instinctive foresight. Dr. Joe Marshalla, author of *Repeatlessness,* believes that oracles just confirm that which we already know to be true, but may be afraid or incapable of admitting or realizing.

The future is such an enticing subject! No wonder fortune-telling has been such a successful business for centuries. Tell me one person who does not want to know what is going to happen? If we only knew when our partner was coming, which business deal was going to work or which way the stock market was going to go, then we wouldn't have to worry. Right? But even with the best fortune telling, there is an aspect that must be taken into account: the future is fluid: plastic, liquid and indefinite. This is what makes life so exciting. The biggest effect comes from the vibration we put towards it, or how we feel about it. That is what is creating avenues for things to happen.

There is still a connotation or association of witchery attached to the word divination. But "divining" for water is not considered a witchery tool. I like to use divination as a guide. Think of sitting around talking to a group of trusted advisors, or a round table of elders or wise beings. It gives you more information to operate from. Psychics have an average percentage rate. Some are accurate 90% of the time, while others vary. There are so many factors which go into the equation. Sometimes familiarity with the subject will interfere with accuracy. If there was one who was 100% accurate, we would know about it. Some use cards or tarot decks, some use information from guides and some use crystals. But even the best use a variety of tools. Each one finds what works for them and even then there is usually a combination of tools.

When someone new comes into my life for any reason, I naturally want to do an intuitive "background" check. I just naturally go to the tools I use to get information. I realize that the information is just that: information to guide me. Using these tools is not putting someone into a box, but they can suggest guidance about how I proceed in fortifying my intuition.

The Pendulum

Ancient, simple and quick. I can keep it in my purse and take it out when I have a yes or no question. Pendulums can be created from crystals, rocks, metal or other objects that have the capacity to attract and hold vibrational energy. Different crystals have different energetic powers including healing, clarity and offering serenity. Typically they are suspended from chains or strings. It's important, as with any divination tool, that the instrument be "coded" to its owner. Sometimes people create unique rituals to bond with their instruments including chants, prayers, meditation and physically touching them.

Decks

Decks are powerful and fun tools to access divine information. The Tarot deck of 72 cards represents the oldest and most widely known type of card divination and include a higher arcana. In the past 20 years, oracle and angel cards have gained extraordinary popularity. They often include magnificent artwork accompanied by specific clues or instructions for the seeker. Whether you use an animal deck or angel cards, they are more direct and a bit less complex than the traditional Tarot. Ultimately, I don't believe Spirit cares which deck you use as long as it personally resonates with you. I particularly love Sonia Choquette's "Ask Your Guides" deck and several decks from Angel Therapist, Doreen Virtue.

Osho Zen Tarot

I use this online deck when I am on the Internet and I want more of an in-depth and instant teaching. I like to do the four card spread and ask about relationships at osho.com

I-Ching Book of Changes

What a magnificent tool! The I-Ching is a Chinese book of ancient origin consisting of 64 interrelated hexagrams along with commentaries attributed to Confucius. The hexagrams, originally used for divination, embody Taoist philosophy by describing all nature and human endeavor in terms of the interaction of yin and yang.

I have friends who commit to and live by the I-Ching. If they do a reading they will alter the course of their life based on what they learn. This is another tool best done ceremonially as the information is rich and cannot be absorbed quickly; it should be read again and again for full understanding. The interpretations reveal multiple levels of complexity.

The Universal DJ

This is an instant, profound and entertaining tool. It seems to work better when you are in the flow than those times when you are not. All you do is put your iPod on shuffle and then pay attention to the songs that come up. Uncanny.

The romance with this process started on my birthday a few days ago. I blocked out the world and completely plugged into music. I hit "shuffle" on my iTunes so that the Universal DJ could do its thing and play songs that matched the vibration I was in– profound love, bliss, private revolution and sacred soulfulness. With a soundtrack of songs like "War" by Lennon and "Early in the Morning" by Doyle Bramhall II, I was no longer an appreciator of deeply connected music, I was an extension, an amplification of this holy vibration.

The playlist kept getting better as the day went on, taking me deeper and deeper. Wrapped up or encoded in music is every human emotion, every heart-quaking desire, every bone-splitting pain, every love-tendered salve; in other words the full human experience.

Music is at the heart of inspiration. If I were to say that it is everything I would not be far from the truth. Music connects us all. It is the universal language. It is the cosmic language as well. Everything is just vibration and music is vibration. It moves us. It never fails to inspire us.

Vibration is the future of healing and all science.

Sometimes when I am deep in the flow, I cannot even listen to music. It touches me too much and I just cry.

The Internet

Everything has consciousness. Every atom, every cell of the body, every rock. There is nothing that doesn't have consciousness because that is all there is.

I witness the consciousness of the Internet frequently. I'm not talking about artificial intelligence, I'm talking about connections that have been made that are so random and so auspicious that they cannot be accidental. I remember being resistant to Facebook. For the first six months I would talk about how I would not use it because it took out the face-to-face aspect communication and the flow that happens naturally. I mean the universe has been operating without it for eons. Why would we need it now? So, I resisted. Then as an author, it became a medium I could not ignore. So I dove in, hesitantly. I also had to deal with my programming that privacy should be protected at all costs. I wasn't crazy about connecting with every single person I went to high school with.

After about three months I started seeing things that convinced me. I found friends that I DID want to re-connect with, which lead to new avenues in my life. Amazing. There really is no excuse anymore for not connecting with people.

We have come to the age of transparency. This is a concept that troubled me because I felt that the loss of privacy could create either more "big brother" in my life or a lack of individuality or I could become a target for uninvited energies. But I am seeing that there is a very powerful and positive aspect to it, and that is. . . that we can consolidate our lives. We can integrate our different personas, and integration is always positive. In the past, it was important to have a business persona and then a private persona. Essentially, all that does is create more separation and work for us.

Magic

This word raises people's eyebrows. Maybe the word is magic in itself. There are so many different interpretations of what magic is. The most common interpretation is a trick or an illusion using some sort of deception, as in a magic show. I'm not talking about this kind of magic. There is another definition that states that magic is the "human control of supernatural agencies or the forces of nature." I use the word magic in this context. And also let me be clear that I don't believe in magic. Magic just IS, whether we believe in it or not. The ancient ways are being remembered strongly and are appearing in new forms.

Magic comes with its own lore. The Internet is the new "witches' cauldron" and the wizards and witches are the healers, light-workers, goddesses, muses and angels walking among us. How does magic work? It works on "mystery technology" or the divine hand at work always. It is not illusion; it is the miracles of this divine play being performed right in front of our eyes, complete with surprises and suspended disbelief. It is awe-inspiring and it happens on a daily basis.

My personal definition of magic is working in concert with the supernatural energies of natural law. The energy of the universe is mysterious and magical, we just have to see it and call it like it is. When a miracle happens, we never cry "magic." But isn't that what it is?

Here's an example of the Internet as a manifestation tool. I have been writing about Pan in my blog. I wrote one day about how Pan was my new boyfriend. Several days later I am sitting in a coffee shop and guess who walks in the door? Pan. He was even wearing a unicorn t-shirt.

I say, "Hi Pan!" and my friend introduces me as a muse. He invites me to lunch and we'll just let the rest be a mystery.

Another example just this very second happened. A woman who was sitting next to me at a café in Sedona walked in the door and sat down near me.

"Magic!" she proclaims.

Then I ask her what she means and she says that she went outside and looked at the red rocks. Upon seeing them, she had the best idea come to her.

"I was just writing about magic," I reply.

"Oh you believe in that?" she asked suspiciously.

"Yes, I don't believe in it, it just IS. And by the way, you obviously do too!" She had gone outside and merged with the supernatural forces of nature and participated in the release of magic.

Several months ago I rented the movie "The Mists of Avalon." As I watched the movie I became flooded with deep feelings of remembrance. I cried at the sight of Merlin. I felt like I was looking at my people. I felt sad for all the people who looked at the world of Avalon as "make believe." I remembered what it felt like to have a close connection to nature. I understood why we had become who we are as a society, yet I was still sad.

As I watched the movie I realized that Avalon actually existed. The mists are the dimensions one has to cross to arrive to the island or state of magic. As Paganism was wiped out, so were many of the old ways.

Observation

I love the law of physics which says "that which you observe is altered." Well, to me that is the law of consciousness. Sometimes I will just watch and listen to a client. That act alone can alter everything. If I am already holding space for transformation to take place and I observe from that perspective, then observation can be potent.

Play

So many of us have forgotten how to play. It's not our fault. For most of our lives our thoughts have been sequestered: to perform, to produce, to study, to make money. We don't get time for our own thoughts and as we know, owning our own thought real estate is a great luxury and one of the last frontiers.

The most expensive real estate on the planet is in your head.

Without that, you cannot play. You have to clear some room on the table to start another project. Play needs space. You cannot play without being in the present moment. It's impossible because play is the present moment held in the suspended vibration of creativity. My favorite word for play is leela: a Sanskrit word for the grand play that is this existence.

But if your mind is totally filled with task oriented thoughts or the habitual reviewing of your to-do list, no play can get in. Play is when you stop and flirt (as in smile and share some love) with the person at the grocery store because your mind isn't stressing out about how to figure out how to write a proposal when you get home. Your mind is free, clear, relaxed and available to the joy of the moment.

A person that forgets how to play has lost himself. He or she is probably not living an authentic life because a piece of them is lost, playing a role. Ironically enough, I recently had a conversation with a professional athlete who "plays" professionally. He complained about his struggle to be relaxed and playful in his life. I thought how ironic it is that such a respected professional "player" doesn't know how to play. He's too busy performing and playing the role. In his defense, there are many people who are just serious-natured. They have to work at letting go and bringing out their childlike experimentation with life.

Sex is play.

It is not performance and doesn't have to be any certain way. It is just playing, experimenting and enjoying: a physical conversation.

You can incorporate play into your daily life by taking the time to just have a mischievous thought. It's as simple as that, whatever that means for you.

The benefit of play is a balanced life. Play is part of your vibrational diet. You want to have comic relief. There is medicine in laughter, enjoyment and appreciation but play is a letting go. Play is blatantly enjoying life. Play is giving yourself permission to do exactly what you want to do. When you play, you become a mischievous partner to yourself.

Play improves your health, your relationships and your overall quality of life. I think that is why pets are recommended to people who live alone. They engage you in a playful way and bring that energy into your life. You cannot be playful and be in a low vibration.

A relaxed mind is a creative mind.

You go to a higher perspective when you laugh at yourself. You are acknowledging that there's a higher place from which to look at everything and at some point everything is ridiculous and funny. We are all on this ship of fools together.

No matter what is happening, you instantly elevate your consciousness by laughing at "what is." It is going beyond the witness state to what I call the "Wittyness" state.

The highest vibration is love, appreciation and gratitude. It is the ultimate state to live in; it's what we all want. It's what people refer to as peace of mind, a life well lived, enlightenment, deep satisfaction or self-realization. It is constantly sustaining a high vibration without contraction.

The Vibrational Diet

Your vibrational diet is what you feed your six senses. It is everything in your sphere, in your world. The vibrational diet consists of all the vibrations you are exposing yourself to at any given moment. Your thoughts, your feelings, your food, your conversations, your music, your landscape, etc. . . all have a direct affect on your experience and where you are vibrating.

If we are all just energy vibrating, then the path to enlightenment is just a matter of altering our vibrational state by increasing our frequencies to enlightened frequencies. So when we are at higher levels of frequencies we are merging with a larger field of enlightened energy. It is like playing with paint. If you put two of the exact same colors together, they just blend into each other because they are the same. Whatever we match in vibration, meaning whatever we are at the same vibration with, we merge with like finding the secret key to the secret door. This IS the law of attraction. This is why you go into the "feeling" or vibration of what you intend in order to bring yourself up to the correct frequency to merge with. Once you merge, you are that!

For example, you must first become what you are looking for in a potential partner. You cannot attract that which you are not. So you cultivate those qualities you are looking for. As you heal yourself, love yourself, elevate your vibration and feel yourself in this newer vibration, these two frequencies magnetize towards each other until they find each other. That is just what energy does. It seeks its perfect match as well. We have all heard the expression "Be the change you are looking for." And "Be the love you are looking for." If I am looking for a partner, I think "How in the world will I ever find this person? I know they're out there, but they could be anywhere on the planet." Well, guess what? Shift your paradigm to the knowing that as you become what you are looking for (develop virtues) and as you feel this nest (ecstatic vibration) of harmony, meaning living "as if," you will magnetize this energy to you.

Making sounds are literally creating vibration. It has been proven that the sound a cat makes when it purrs actually heals his body five times faster than the normal rate of healing. The same thing applies to the sounds we make. Our "purring" during happiness and physical intimacy has tremendous healing effects on our bodies as well. Just about everything is ingested vibration: food, beauty, music, scents, art, people, nature, environments, surroundings, weather, touch and sound. "The voice itself is a cathedral," says Susan Hale, author of "Sacred Space, Sacred Sound." She adds that ". . . we are sound chambers resonating with the One Song."

When I find my life is not operating at a very high vibration, or in other words when no flow is happening, I first look at what I am ingesting vibrationally.

Questions to help find vibrational harmony:

- What am I eating?
- Who am I spending time with?
- What music am I listening to?
- What am I drawing into my sphere?
- What am I watching on T.V.?
- Am I watching too much depressing news?
- What is my state of organization?
- Where am I spending my time?
- What am I thinking about or obsessing on?
- How am I talking to myself?
- How am I talking to others?
- What am I reading or studying?
- What am I wearing?
- What am I contributing to the flow and what is the flow contributing to me?

10 Ways to raise Your Vibrational Harmony:

I know I need to make some adjustments in my vibrational diet when I lose my shine and lose my excitement about life. Basically I notice when I am not having fun anymore. The first thing I do is address the six senses. What am I hearing, thinking, seeing, ingesting, eating, breathing, smelling and touching?

Once I start to pinpoint the toxins, as subtle or loud as they may be, I begin to make some changes. I may put on some classical music and go spend time with the roses in the garden. For me, that is like an espresso shot of raising my vibration. Looking at color and beautiful things is a form of vibrational food. Seeing something wonderful is food. An uplifting movie is food. What you look at is food. I will think about who I've been talking to and what vibration they have been feeding me. I will think about how I've been speaking to myself, the vibration of self-talk, or how I'm speaking to others. I will think about where I'm spending my time. Am I planning my day to be in traffic or in a more harmonious flow? Am I in nature enough? It's about just being aware of everything. When you're feeding yourself vibrational crap, try a few changes and see what happens.

I walked into a gym recently around five o'clock and the vibe was aggressive like a pack of wild dogs had just been released. People were grinding it out on the cardio machines and the look on their on their faces was scary like the wicked witch of the west peddling with Toto on the back. I turned around, left and opted for a run around Town Lake, knowing that nature was a better diet than aggression. Birds and trees over hamsters on treadmills with cell phones.

You don't have to think whether or not you're in a no flow situation or feeding yourself a poor vibrational diet:

It just feels bad.

You walk into a room and you know whether if feels bad or good; there is no thinking to it. There is a health food grocery store in L.A. that has the worst music, the worst lighting, the skinniest aisles and is completely over-crowded. Of all places, this should be a "feel good" place but it's not. You walk into a situation and you know in an instant, just like a kid. Slow it down and notice your instant childlike response:

I don't like this or I do like this. . .
or
This feels good or it doesn't. . .

We're not always in control of our environments. Sometimes we need to be where we don't want to be and we don't have a choice. We all have to accept and surrender to certain environments and circumstances. That is when our tools come in handy. We can always control our thoughts. So at a minimum, controlling how we think about what we're doing and raising our internal vibration to one of calm acceptance can change things.

Live "As If"

Our frequencies can change, elevate and leave our minds behind. You may still think that you have far to go when in actuality, you may already be there. You just don't have the language, the reflection, the paradigm shift to validate your new position. Example: I live a life of joy and yet my mind still plays the trick on me that I have not gone far enough or done enough or am not enough.

I am already vibrating at the state that knows this is not true, but the mind still plays the old tapes.

As we climb the mountain, we have to stop and look down every now and then to see how far we have come.

Passion

Passion is defined as any powerful emotion or feeling such as love or hate. It is a strong or extravagant enthusiasm for anything. It is really just a fancy word for desire. It is like desire with a turbo-charge behind it. You can feel passionate about anything you love. It has that extra horse-power which sends out a strong signal to the universe with a loud speaker attached announcing "THIS IS WHAT I WANT!" That is more powerful than effort or hard work because that is sending out the signal that is seeking its match.

I love the fact that passion is desire on steroids. We all are in love with people who are passionate because passion is magnetizing. I recently saw a solo violinist perform in an old church in Venice, Italy. The young man was so passionate about what he was playing he threw his whole body into it. We in the audience felt like voyeurs watching an intimate private act. He had abandoned himself and was in the throws of passion as he was making love to his violin. In return the music was making love to him as well. It was a scene of artistic lovemaking and we were all enthralled. Who doesn't like witnessing passion, especially when combined with talent and virtuosity? Isn't that what makes any artist worth watching?

This is what makes the performing arts so fulfilling to watch, the written arts so engaging to read and the visual arts so thrilling to see. Anything can be imbued with passion from graffiti on the street to the way someone cooks a meal.

Seeing someone completely swept away in passion is irresistible. An athlete, a dancer, a singer. In fact the more out of control the more mesmerizing. Think about Steven Tyler singing in the early days or Swami Jimmy Hendrix on guitar or Yoyo Ma on the cello. You know that you are witnessing something sacred because you are. It is the artist in his flow. It is divine. It is what some of us live for.

This is one of the reasons I am in love with the electric guitar. It is the passionate instrument that rocks my world. And it is a mainstay of my vibrational diet!

The Electric Guitar

I was having the kind of day that felt like a quicksand bath. I had a horrible headache, felt clumsy in my body and was wondering why I thought I could ever write a book. I stumbled around town and then finally gave up all thoughts of working, working out or eating healthy. Instead I went to a theater and saw the movie "It Might Get a Loud" featuring Jimmy Page (Led Zeppelin), Jack White (White Stripes, The Raconteurs) and The Edge (U2).

Ten minutes into it, I realized that half of the time we are hungry, it is not for food. It is for a higher vibration, which you can sometimes get from food, but not always. This movie fed my being as an artist, a creative person, a lover of music, a lover, a rebel, a student, a teacher, an ageless creature and a spirit. It passed the heart-leaping test 100%, and my heart was lurching forward at the communion with others who live for, and on, inspiration.

An elegantly smoldering and musically intoxicating Jimmy Page talked about how passion begins as a creative spark, catches fire and then burns bright. Everything else pales by comparison. It is an energetic addiction.

Why am I so in love with the electric guitar these days?

It's the amplification.

Artists have a deep need to connect with others. It doesn't matter if it's through music, words, painting or circus balloons. But the electric guitar is the physical instrument of amplification; pure vibration loud enough to blow your hair back. I just can't get enough.

PASSION EXERCISE

What is it that you get completely lost in? What can you do today that you love so much you may look like a fool doing? If you are having trouble thinking about it, here are a few prompts to get you started:

- Put on your favorite music in the car and SCREAM SING to it.

- Watch your favorite sports team and really yell for your team.
- Find your favorite poem and reread it.
- Rent a movie that you know will make you cry because it is ridiculously romantic.
- Write a very romantic letter that you will never send to your perfect partner—real or imagined.
- Play an Ennio Morricone score while you go for a walk downtown or watch a sunset.
- Flip through images of Caravaggio renaissance paintings while listening to Beethoven.

Sometimes some of the silliest things can stir our passion. A fresh crayon, a box of paints, a bloom on a tree, a spider web or anything that enraptures.

We want to feel. That is what being alive is all about, yet sometimes we do everything to avoid feeling.

CHAPTER 19

THE LANGUAGE OF MUSES: EXSTATICS

I cannot tell you how many times I have heard people say, "I don't even have the words to describe this feeling. . . " or "what is the word for. . . ?" and "why is this?" It's because we are experiencing new feelings, new energies and new fertile ground in this emerging paradigm.

We hear about the new paradigm but what does it really mean? I'm no expert, but I can tell you my experience. I AM living in a new world. Right now. Nothing is the same. I am not the same. Things simply don't work the same way.

To me, the shift is because of new energies that somehow appeared on our planet. There are many people who can speak insightfully on the nature of these energies and where they come from. One common thread in defining this new paradigm is a shift in consciousness on a planetary level, as defined by Dr. Joe Marshalla.

The current transition we find ourselves in, referred to by many as the change, the shift or the new paradigm, is nothing more and nothing less than an evolutionary step in human consciousness. This step in consciousness is not characterized by a single event but to the contrary is more a release of the multitude of constraints, rules and conditions that we have put on ourselves as a species, which has generated the very separation consciousness and division of ideologies among us. The new paradigm can be characterized as a return to our awareness of our true nature beyond our identification with the mind. For all that is beautiful, magnificent, peaceful, loving and the quintessential expression of the perfection of love and harmony, is who in fact, we are. And all that is not working on this planet, all that would be characterized as awful, disrespectful, mean, destructive, or moreover all that would be characterized as evil is in fact, a product of the mind. So the new paradigm appears to be a process through which we are realizing personal responsibility for all that is happening on the planet, the recognition that the earth and its resources are the common heritage of all its inhabitants, and lastly an acceptance and knowing that all life, not just human, represents a singularity in its multi-faceted expression. It's important to realize that this shift is an ongoing process. That is to say there is not a moment that will occur when it is complete. It is a process that has been happening for millions of years and will continue to happen for millions more. Therefore, in acknowledging this shift, one becomes an active participant whereby their every thought, action and response to the world is one that is guided by a commitment to uplift and nurture all life on the planet and contribute to the collective as a whole. In this acknowledgment and active participation we realize that everything that has ever happened was absolutely necessary, required and needed to occur so that we could transcend. Therefore, animosity, anger, revenge, greed and selfishness are quickly becoming modalities of the past. And love, harmony, selflessness, compassion, understanding, empathy, generosity, equanimity, joy, celebration, unity and the true moment to moment experiential awareness of our oneness shall be the common principle guiding all our lives and decisions.

George Humphrey, economist, author and documentarian, states that:

As humans we are constantly experiencing many different cycles -the easiest to understand are the seasons: Spring, Summer, Fall and Winter. Indeed, what we call 'Life' is constant movement of energy in cyclical patterns. The ancient Rishis of the Himalayan Mountains knew that the earth, and society, are totally interconnected by subtle energies, and by understanding and living in harmony with these energies we as humans could progress on our Spiritual Journey. These Sages knew that for the last six thousand years our planet and our society have been dominated by a convoluted Patriarchal energy that is out of touch with nature and motivated by greed, control and illusion. They also prophesied in the Vedas that at this very moment in the time we are living would usher in a new vibration of consciousness, sustainability and co-operation. Wow, that is cool. Quite clearly one does not need to talk with a Yogi to understand that there is 'something wrong' and that our society is treating this planet in a totally unsustainable fashion -this awareness can be a pretty bitter pill to swallow. However, more and more people are waking up in faith and awareness that we can heal our planet and ourselves -some people call this the New Paradigm. The 'New Para-

digm' is really pretty simple and really not that new -it basically says:

1. We are only 'Victims' if we allow ourselves to be -snap out of it, and reclaim your innate sovereignty and divinity

2. This is not a 'Dress Re-Hearsal,' each person's thoughts and actions are now magnified in manifestation

3. *Life is a Game -So Play it Well.* With this game there are certain *Universal Laws*: a. *The Law of Attraction,* b. *The Law of Conscious Creation*, c. *The Law of Allowance* (the hard one), d. *The Law of Balance and Harmony*, and e. *The Law of Repeatlessness.* By truly taking personal responsibility and really understanding our own divinity and connection with all Creation we will play by the *Universal Laws* and move into the new cycle with ease. No one said this transition was going to be simple, but just keep practicing and loving, and remember it is all a game, so play it well!

At times, I see a shift in my world through the eyes of everyone around me. I witness separation beginning to dissolve and a lighter brighter energetic field around me. I notice a return to unlimited possibilities, which probably needs a new word. Let's call it **Forever Sky**. That's where the limited reaches into the unlimited; the highly desirable state of "I didn't even know that I didn't even know." Let's call this **The Delicious Unknown**. I feel deep changes at work, all the way down to the core of the earth. And they are ALL good, in the long run.

So while this may not be a completely new set of words, it is a beginning way to speak about this new territory we have arrived in. To be able to express a little more about what we are now feeling and experiencing, a language of **exstatics, atmospherics** and **gasmics** has been created.

Exstatics is the name of this new language that brings in a whole new octave of words that help us to express these higher frequencies: these heightened states of joy, bliss and co-creation.

Atmospherics is the name for words that help us to express a new level of sensuality. As we become more intimate now, we breathe in the rarified air of our heightened senses.

Gasmics are the words that help us to describe our accelerated AHA! moments.

So far language has just evolved. Now we have come to a time when we are able to evolve it and as a result evolve ourselves at an accelerated pace.

The Language of Business

Winning feels good. It feels really good to create win/win situations. The more exponential you can make the win/win/win/win, etc, the greater the thrill. The power of the win scale is unlimited and the elation needs a new language to describe this new celebration of winning.

I call this state **Windom**. It is the art of being conscious of every possible win at every moment. For example, you are going to get a coffee. The windom begins with the decision of which coffee shop to go to, maybe you choose one that sells fair trade coffee (a global win), one that uses recycled materials (an environmental win) and maybe you even ride your bike. Maybe your favorite barista is working who lets you know that she puts love into your coffee (a consciousness elevating win) and you let her know how much you appreciate that (a gratitude win.)

Another example may be a new business venture. Every decision considers how many wins can be accomplished. It may be as simple as giving credit to everyone who actually deserves credit or it may involve profit sharing, charitable contributions, mentoring, sponsoring, etc.

The Language of Work

One of the best things I learned was to be happy with what I have. Period. I have made lists for what I can be grateful for which is a powerful activity. It is commonly known that gratitude has magnetizing power and attracts opportunities.

I also learned that in this new paradigm, community, cooperation and co-creation have **No Collar**.

OK, it gets even better. . . because in this era of no collar, it is about finding our roles. Not the right job, but the right role. Even the ancients have always said that every person has a very special purpose, unique only to him or her. Haven't we all desperately wished to have our purpose lined up with our gift, which then lines us up with the perfect amount of money we desire?

I am feeling that this mutual alignment phenomenon is happening now on the planet and will start happening more frequently. I am the perfect example. I am now working as a modern muse. My gift is to see people in their highly polished state and then take them there through inspiration and ideas. I love to create, constantly. So what job is this? Well it has no name, because it is not a job, it is a **role**.

The Language of Play

This new paradigm that is happening NOW is all about community, co-operation and co-creation, which is the **New Communion**. What is becoming apparent to me now is this:

The fun is in the co-creation.

We no longer have to do it all ourselves! There is usually someone right under your nose who is the perfect co-creator.

The Language of Love

How much can you be in love? In every second? **Crushdom** is taken to a new level when we literally make the world our lover. What if whoever was in front of you in THIS moment was your greatest love (not physically speaking)? The dry cleaner lady, the barista, your client, whoever is in the frame. What if whatever is in front of you at THIS moment was something you truly loved? A meal, a river, a firefly, a computer, a bed-ridden elder person who needs his diaper changed. What if we could live with that level of profundity? What if the world really was my boyfriend and I could never shrink love down to just one thing or one person but to the one thing or one person right now, right in front of me? What if you just wanted to be in love in every single second? I do.

The Language of Pleasure and Intimacy

What if we had a language of ooohs and aaahs and long sighs? And growls and purrs and hisses and roars? And piratey aaaarghs! And hums and yums?

I call the energetics of sensuality, **Atmospherics**. Atmospherics are states of intoxication. They exist in a complete heirarchy. They get more intense as two lovers get physically closer. The only action required is that both slow down enough to feel the atmosphere changing.

About a foot away, you have entered the atmosphere of a heavenly body (your lover). Speaking takes on a different tone in this rare-aired atmosphere. As the magnetizing energy of this heavenly body draws you close, everything vibrates higher into disorientation, very similar to intoxication.

When the molecules of your breath actually mingle, the divine (the breath) becomes manifest as it re-enters the body. A divine alchemy of spirit into form occurs. Then the kiss, watch out! The moistened genitalia skin of the lips makes contact, and a whole other atmosphere is entered. And on it goes, through the atmospherics, all of which orbit around the heart.

There is nothing to say about sex except that we can always go deeper, which incidentally applies to everything. The ancient teachings of Tantra taught that one of the secrets to the enjoyment of sex is: Enjoyment! What if you could dive in so deep into the moment, you actually were transported? Say you are touching your lover. Instead of thinking about what he or she is feeling you are so aware of every sensation coming through your fingertips from the temperature of his or her skin to the texture of your own skin, to the speed at which you are moving your fingers, to the weight of the touch – so that you become completely lost. You are diving in so deep to the pleasure that there is no future, no orgasm to go for, and no thought or judgment about what anybody is doing. It is just play and this is one of the states of exstatics.

The Language of Synchronicities and Magic

This is the lost language of magic and the old ways. Many of these words and insights died along with the goddess cultures. The awareness and usage of these mysteries were the only elements required to keep them alive. They faded as the pagan communities were replaced by religious institutions and the practitioners were persecuted, forced underground to keep them alive in mystical sects. There was a movement away from the energies of Mother Earth and the inherent magic of nature.

Magic is really just another dimension. Just like Avalon and Camelot, it existed as a construct that can be accessed through the mists or layers of consciousness. These dimensions can still be accessed. As the veil becomes thinner and thinner in this new paradigm, magic will be much more visible.

Maybe you have noticed an increase in synchronicities. The right person showing up at the right time. The ideal situation just falling into your lap beyond your wildest imagination. I have even noticed that there are multiple synchronicities like three people showing up at the right time and right place or multiple events, one after the other. Well, this is the new way as we all fall into our roles and more into divine alignment. It still doesn't mean that we aren't shocked by their intense aha! moments. This is the language of **gasmics**; exploding moments of delight, surprise, beauty, connection and awe, that leave us momentarily speechless.

At the heart of magic is the great mystery, the divine hand at work always.

The Language of Self-Talk

How do we stop those voices in our head? I don't know, but we can start to replace them with the language of self-love.

Negative self-talk, shoulds and guilt are universal. But, what if we gave ourselves permission to follow our desires? What if we change the word permission to promission and did not need anyone's approval? For example, "I really should take that job" becomes "I give myself **promission** to not take that job that I don't really want."

Another cause of great suffering is how we speak to ourselves when we perceive ourselves to be rejected. What if we replace rejection with **not-a-fit**? For example you have a romantic connection with someone who never calls you back. You could tell yourself that you are rejected or you could just tell yourself that it was **not-a-fit**.

Sometimes fear, doubt and self-hatred just take over. When we are not remembering who we really are. Sometimes the only way out of this misery is to assume what the mystics call "the witness." What if the witness observing this misery had a sense of humor? You could observe yourself believing some crap, have a sense of humor about it and become the **Wittyness**.

The Language of Community

What if there were angels walking among us? I'm just going to assume that there are because I see so many people finding their roles and offering their assistance. I see the divine at work, even though we don't usually use angelic words to describe the goodness that is out there. These people, the angels, light workers, healers and agents of positive change who know who they are, are what I call the community of **The Featherhood**.

I want to make a movie about a band of sexy, glamorous people, fully living the human experience who find that there is nothing that excites them anymore than to do things that truly help people. To me, the new spiritual doesn't look spiritual at all anymore.

The Language of Enlightenment

It's funny how I have spent decades longing and searching for enlightenment. I was the seeker's seeker, traveling all over the world, even following a spiritual master for six years. I must say, I truly loved every aspect of the search and each step of the way. But lately, a strange thing has occurred. The word "enlightenment" rarely comes up on my radar screen. Why? Because what I crave and long for now more than anything is to be in this magnificent flow or **alignment**. This is not a new word, but the best description I have of how the energy feels.

When I am in Alignment,
nothing more is needed,
as it is heaven on earth,
the New Communion,
doing what I love most every second,
playing my role with Windom,
in the state of Crushdom,
in awe of the Gasmics
and lost in the Delicious Unknown.

OLD PARADIGM	vs	NEW PARADIGM
Limitations	vs	Forever Sky
Fear of the unknown	vs	The Delicious Unknown
Achievement	vs	Windom
Job	vs	Role
Rugged Individualism	vs	Co-Creation
Community	vs	The New Communion
Rejection	vs	Not-a-fit
Witness Consciousness	vs	Wittyness
Cinderella Compex	vs	Crushdom
Sensuality	vs	Atmospherics
Aha! Moments	vs	Gasmics
Synchronicities	vs	Sparkling Intersections

ABOUT MUSING

For those who may have a passion for musing others there are certain qualities of musing to explore. These techniques and insights go beyond the scope of traditional coaching and incorporate an intuitive, spontaneous and creative approach: a fun, non-spiritual approach.

We are all muses to each other. There is always someone you are inspiring or who is inspiring you. A motorcycle ride late at night, being in nature, a long car drive, sitting in a sacred spot, playing with animals. Music is a universal muse. There is no one who cannot be inspired or touched by music. Hence the word, Muse-ic. Everyone has an entry point into the creative world. This is musing yourself.

Inspiring others comes naturally to some people. Performers, poets, dancers, musicians and artists are all muses for others, but even their inspiration comes from another unseen source. When we follow the path of the Muse, we arrive in a state where past, present and future co-exist in a brilliant framework of understanding and expression. In other words, to inspire we must be inspired. To be inspired, we must inspire. It is a spiritual co-creative mobius that demands we pay attention to both the muse within and the inspiration we deliver.

If you have a calling to be a professional muse, it helps if musing lines up with the trifecta or CDP.

- You have a true heart's desire for this. Your heart will leap at the idea of even considering doing something like this.

- You have a talent for this. This is a gift that you have and you just do it naturally.

- It serves the highest. This means that it is your purpose and therefore is done with the intention to serve. You must truly love bringing out the creative, the artist in others. For some this is hard because in some ways you are behind the scenes. You may be giving brilliant ideas that are going to make someone millions, sparking the idea for the next blockbuster movie or brainstorming the next technological breakthrough.

You have to give these without attachment as to how they will fare out in the world.

You are a conduit and things are meant to flow through you like currency.

It is energy that needs to flow. You contribute without feeling like you are going to receive credit. Acknowledgment may not come. If you co-create something magnificent, the person you are working with may not want to credit a muse. Success does funny things to people. You have to do this knowing that you may be a background support player.

CHAPTER 20

CREATING YOUR STOREFRONT

Once I committed to being in alignment with my purpose and my gift, I wanted to create my "storefront." This is a term that Karen Bishop uses in her "What's up on Planet Earth.com" writings. She sees our storefronts as how we market out new roles. To me, this meant actually making a living with CDP.

Here's how it played out for me. I always say that I have had many lifetimes in one body. I have been a mother, a nationally recognized designer, a jewelry designer and manufacturer, a fashion designer, a writer, a dancer, an artist, a treasure hunter, a disciple to a spiritual master and a yoga teacher. And so, I had already done these things. I wanted to do something beyond all this; something that completely excited me and deeply satisfied me.

As I took time off to write and explore my "next," I noticed how much of my time was spent talking to people. There were at least ten people in my life who would call and say something along the lines of, "I need a Giselle fix." There was a lawyer, a real estate agent, a university professor, a student, a marketing consultant, several business owners, a yoga instructor and several speakers. I found myself spending lots of time in coffee shops talking to people. I was just going from one to another. Usually at the meetings, I would counsel, guide, share an insight, help remove a block, provide clarity and give spiritual advice that would come to me as a "knowingness." But mostly I had ideas. I would see where this person could go and I could see ideas that he or she had never considered. I always have ideas. I felt like I was constantly going around to meetings being a fountain of ideas. But it wasn't just me having ideas. I was co-creating with these people. We were birthing all these ideas together. AND IT WAS FUN. We created a vortex of up-lifting, creative energy. We left feeling like we just had sex and needed a cigarette. It didn't matter the topic: it could be finance, real estate, technology, relationships, careers, speaking topics. . . anything. So what was I? A professional coffee shop-hopper and idea fountain?

It was about that time that I met a healer who gave me another clue. He asked me how much I charged for my healings.

"What?" was my response. "I'm not a healer and I don't see clients," I added.

He laughed at this.

"Sure you do. You just have all your clients in your friend line. Your life will change when you hang your shingle and take everyone out of your friend line and put them in your client line." I thought about it and realized that I was spending an incredible amount of time helping people break through barriers, overcome obstacles and re-imagine their lives. I was an advisor to many of my own friends including massage therapists, yoga teachers, creative instructors and more. So why not make it an equitable exchange: money for services? And oddly enough, the services became more valuable to my "friends" upon hiring me. And ultimately, the new paradigm is designed to help support all of us in our work to elevate the planet.

This started the wheels turning. Now was the time to do for myself what I was doing for everyone else. Bring my "next" out into the world, hang my shingle and start seeing people.

This of course brought up all kinds of fear and worthiness issues:

- Can I really see people?
- Do I really have something to offer?
- What if I am a fraud?

- What will I actually do?
- How will people find me?
- How will I charge?
- What should I charge?

Initially, I approached this as if I were a consultant and came up with an hourly fee. Since some of my potential clients were yoga teachers and some were high-level executives, I set my fees on a sliding scale. After working with a CEO for a few months, he suggested I come up with a rate to muse the entire company. This involved making myself available to whomever wanted to see me in hourly sessions. I came up with a monthly rate for this since it took at least half of my working time. This also paid a little more than half my bills. This job lasted almost six months which gave me time to seek other individuals.

Unlike coaching where your relationships extend over many months and goals are met, musing seems to happen in bursts. Many times I will see a client about three times. When I am doing my job, it feels like I am igniting people and then providing realistic recommendations to get where they are going. Usually we have the fully fleshed idea of where they are going; their new role, new job, new business name, new look, new life or maybe just some refined tweaking to what they are doing. This work can be fast as inspiration is the fuel.

Don't Quit Your day Job Yet

For many, pursing your role is a process. Especially if you are blazing some new trails and there are no traditional models to follow. But it's like starting any new business venture. The reality is that it takes time and planning.

In my case, I had the good fortune of not having to worry about financial survival initially. At that time, I had a financial cushion sufficient enough to allow me to jump into musing. However, I have started a business before with absolutely no cushion and barely enough gas in my tank to get to a meeting. This high-risk scenario is very motivating!

My next step was to name my role. One has to name one's self, call one's self something, create something for people to find them as we build our new "storefronts".

I went through every iteration of counselor/healer names such as transformation consultant, change agent, transformation coach and idea fountain, but none of them seemed to fit, just like Cinderella's slipper. I tried putting myself into those shoes grudgingly. Maybe the closest thing would be life coach, but I didn't focus on goals, success models or strategy. I wasn't a guide because I'm not a spiritual teacher. I wasn't a psychic because I don't predict the future, although I do work from intuition. All of these things were missing one major element: my heart did not leap at the sound of it.

CHAPTER 21

ROLE CONSCIOUSNESS VS. JOB CONSCIOUSNESS

Job consciousness was the part of the process for me when I was ready for my "next" and looked around and didn't see anything that fit. I was looking for a place to fit in. Anytime we are looking for a place to fit in, we are in trouble. So I had to create something that fit me. It's approaching our right work from a whole different angle. Maybe there is a job that fits what you do. I think a lot of us are going to have to create our jobs in the future, or our ROLES.

So pretend that you are in college and you have to choose a major. You look at the course catalog and don't see anything even remotely resembling what you are interested in. There are a few things, but not really. You don't see a class for exactly what you are interested in. You don't see a listing for a major that reads:

"Doing exactly what you want to be doing at all times. In fact, if you don't do exactly what you want to do at all times you will fail this course of study. Involves magic, believing in yourself, playing, taking time off, being creative, delivering messages from the universe and helping people shine their brightest. Optional studies: unicorn riding, impatient behavior, being a social butterfly and staying in divine alignment." No, I did not see this course description but if I had, I would have made it my major.

I am beginning to see that there is a role for everyone. A very special role for everyone. So imagine, in this paradigm what it would be like if more and more people found their "groove," their special gift wanting to be expressed. If enough people were doing what they were meant to do and what they loved doing, maybe there would be people doing all the things we didn't want to do.

Imagine!

Some Obstacles to finding Your Life's purpose

The biggest obstacle is when people have trouble making the shift from job consciousness to role consciousness. Let's look at it from a practical standpoint. Say Brook is a make-up artist who is looking to change her life. She is ready for her "next," but doesn't really know what it is. She knows she loves working with people, she loves skin and the beauty industry, she loves travel and she loves going out at night. She also loves being in the limelight and doing media appearances. If she were to find this course in a college catalog it would read: "Play with make-up with your friends. Help everyone look beautiful, experiment with new styles and talk about all the new beauty services that are out there right now from lasers to botox to surgery. Then, go experiment, get some of these services and see how they work. See how they work on other people. Travel to different towns and experiment in other cities. Put on glamorous party clothes and then socialize, meet people, go to happy hours in other cities as well and talk about what you want to talk about regarding the beauty world. Be glamorous. And then receive recognition and compensation for your contribution to this field."

As she reads this course description, she gets excited. "What is this job? I want it!!" This is actually how she begins the shift into role consciousness. There isn't really a job like this that she knows of. But she knows that she plays the role of inspiring women and men who want to take the next step in skincare and just don't have the time, the knowledge or the aesthetic means to get there themselves. This role is a lot like a make-up artist but a make-up artist usually just works in a salon and sees people as they come in. Rarely is there travel or experimentation with all the latest skin services.

What about starting her own business where she checks out all the millions of options available to us in skin care and cosmetic services and finds out what is good out there? That way, I wouldn't have to waste time going from one place to another, to find who has the lowest price and who is the best. Also, I want someone to tell me what options are available. The industry changes every week with new technologies for anti-aging and skin rejuvenation. Then I want her to set all this up for me. She could find out about the latest treatments and who is doing them and what they could do for me. She could even get them done so I see how it would look. What if she became a "Face Specialist"? What if she became "The Plumper Expert"? What if she had a website and constantly posted this information? And what if the people offering these services paid her to come into their studios and check out what they had to offer so she would write about them? What if she did this in other towns? What if she had a YouTube channel and posted videos on what she found out there? What if she had her own internet show? What if she also talked about how to love the beauty you already possess as well? What if she shared about the years when she was obese and how it felt? Or how she lost the weight? And how she still carried around "fat consciousness" even though she had lost the weight? This is how she might be more effective in a new role rather than just look for the next job.

Another obstacle to finding our life purpose is our belief system. We may not have an understanding that the universe is here to support us in doing what we are meant to do. We may not trust that what we most want to be doing is exactly what we should be doing. We may not trust that this is a kind, generous and fun-loving universe!

What about finding a partner the same way we find our new roles. Instead of seeing who is out there that we like, why don't we see who fits us. Why don't we make a list of all the qualities that we have and then let the person show up who has the matching ones?

I think there is a partner for everyone. Whenever I feel like I am never going to find my partner, I just go to the mall. I always see a couple of the very oddest people together. And whenever I see a couple like this, I sigh a sigh of relief knowing that there is someone for everyone.

Why is the shift so hard to being our biggest, shiniest selves?

CHAPTER 22

A SESSION WITH A MUSE

Process is a better word than session. In fact it is a 'no process' process. Although the sessions are planned to take about an hour, it is an organic process.

Ideas flow through this process, but not on a schedule. When I work with someone, they are "in my head" so to speak. I used to hear the expression "holding space for someone" and never really knew what it meant. But now I do. It is like keeping someone in your head at all times. I am constantly conscious of them. Everything that comes into my field I filter as something that may or may not apply to them. The door is open for ideas and consciousness to flow through me to them. A session is the time to get together and formally meet face to face. It is usually very casual, over lunch or coffee. Sometimes I will drive by, my client will come out and we will sit in my car for a few minutes and talk, it is all about what they need.

In a sample session with a muse who knows what will happen? We may go swimming, we may go to a movie or a party. We may drink coffee or meet in a certain section at the bookstore or the library. The possibilities are endless. The key component is that it is, Bam! just on target and fruitful.

CHAPTER 23

CASE HISTORY

The Story of a Muse and Her Client.

It was a sunny day and I had to go to the job site. The job was an apartment complex that was undergoing renovation into a condominium. A "condo-conversion" as it was called. I was going to meet with the general contractor about how the job was progressing. A large barrel-chested thirty-something man entered from one of the units, wearing a pink button-down shirt. Kind of a young ship-captain, manly man. We introduced ourselves. I remember looking in his eyes but I more remember him looking at my eyes and seeing something. We talked briefly about the project and then somehow the conversation immediately landed on meditation. I'm not even sure how we got there. But it was acknowledged that we were both "career" meditators and had been practicing meditation for a long time. For some reason, it was important to establish this common thread. We talked some more and then I left.

Several weeks later, I found that I needed to follow up with him on a detail. And thus our weekly conversations began. We had a running dialog concerning real estate and different kinds of deals involving real estate. Then other projects came up in my life where I would need a second opinion regarding a real estate deal and I would find myself calling him and asking his opinion. I saw in him some wonderful qualities that could be brought out and polished. Not to put him in a box, I found him highly intelligent, in the genius geek-nerd category.

One day he was leaning on the balcony rail and I saw a side view of him. While viewing his profile, time stood still. It was like a freeze frame and I saw this aristocratic leader as he stood and surveyed the land below him. I saw a benevolent and purposeful leader who was going to change things.

I also found it interesting that he was a meditator because his energy did not seem to match that of a meditator. His language and actions were fast and sharp, like he was wired on 78 rpms and I was playing at 45 rpms. So as we exchanged information about the real estate market, we would eventually always discuss consciousness. He was all about information.

Over time, we established a weekly rhythm. Before long we saw each other at least once or twice a week, just to exchange information. As I interacted with him, I began to point out to him specific mannerisms which I noticed. One of the first was the way he answered his phone. He was very sharp and brusque, like a robot on too much coffee. I asked if he realized what he sounded like when he answered the phone.

"No, I was not aware, thank you," was his reply.

I would say things in the moment about how he did things, how he presented himself. He always received the observation with gratitude. There was no ego in the way.

We talked over many possible real estate deals. We would look at them, analyze, learn, research and collaborate on assessing different deals. Soon we were looking for deals to do together. Soon we were talking daily. The relationship grew. Deals started happening. Whenever we would get together, the main theme was that of creativity. We would just come up with ideas and solutions. It was always light, fun and spontaneous. It was pure play.

Magic was happening on a daily basis. There was a tremendous flow. Every single time I saw that he was not being who he was meant to be, I would point it out and he would listen without being offended. Every time I saw that he was not matching up to the vision I had of him as a benevolent mogul, I would call him on it. I picked up on everything from the way he did business to the way he spent his time, to the way he was with others to how he treated his body, how he exercised, how he dressed, how he treated his wife, etc.

Sometimes I would meet with him just to let him know how off-track he had become. And he was appreciative of the honesty. I was not afraid to point things out. It just worked and trust was developed.

One day, after I had come out of the closet so to speak, as a professional muse, we just decided to call a spade a spade. I was his muse. We worked out a fee for my services. This accelerated our progress because there was no more trying to define our relationship as partners, friends or what it was that we were. This gave me even more freedom to cultivate those qualities of his that I saw from the beginning. And he was open. But the results of these co-creative sessions were off the chart.

While having coffee at Starbuck's, I was hit with a Theta Burst. That is scientific lingo for a creative burst, true inspiration. It's what I like to eat for breakfast everyday. Anyway we were having a typical conversation about how to change the world when we started talking about how the quickest way to evolve consciousness was to evolve the language. That's when a light went off and a new language was just downloaded into my head right then and there on the spot. I reached for a pen to write as fast as I can before the information disappears.

I frantically leapt out of my seat and asked the next table if anyone had any paper. I was on a time constraint and had to get the info hot out of the oven as it was coming. I asked several people and no one seemed to have any paper. Everyone had a computer, but there was no paper to be found except for the cash register tape or a napkin. So I started writing on a napkin. In about a minute or two, one of the people I had asked for paper was standing there with a red spiral notebook. This stranger had gone to the office store next door and bought one for us: a charming and gallant gesture. It was then that my client and I met his next business partner, a physicist.

It was weeks later that this physicist introduced my client to the CEO of a publicly held company. Before long, my client was bringing little drawings of gadgets he was designing for a new web platform. I would offer my changes and tweaks as we continued to play in our usual fashion.

My client is now the CEO of a division of this company and I am still musing, but now I'm doing it for the whole company.

CHAPTER 24

STAYING IN THE FLOW

The Unflow

I love that incredible feeling when everything is happening perfectly. I am in the perfect place at the perfect time with the perfect surprise presenting itself.

But what about when you are absolutely NOT in the flow? For example, I am in L.A. with a million things I want to get done and I can't even get a rental car to begin my day. The moment has turned into a three-hour nightmare of which I'll spare you the grisly details. It ends with me in tears at Whole Foods trying to eat some sushi as the day continues to spiral into. . . well you get the picture. Even as I am writing this, a large random grey hairball has rolled onto my foot. Ewww!

I say let's juice it up. Circulate money, spread love, share ideas, contribute to the flow. That's what currency is all about. Tell a juicy story, get someone wet with a water hose, give money away to someone on the street corner. Take any ideas you are hoarding and give them away. Become a fountain of love so everyone within a few feet of you will get splashed.

Then I realized something. It is impossible not to be in the flow. Life is a flow. It's just that my flow happened to look like RESISTANCE today. Maybe all this resistance is guiding me perfectly, beyond what I can see. I am so quick to judge frustration as bad, when it is just information flowing towards me, just the same as when so called "good things" are happening. The flow is learning to love the full human experience without the judgment of good or bad.

HOW TO GET BACK IN THE FLOW EXERCISE
The Now Screen
What if:

. . . what you saw in front of you was defined as YOUR SCREEN? It is your movie that you are watching every second. Wait, let's get even more specific. Your body is a projector and your eyes are the rays that are projecting the moving image. Everything that you see, in your field of vision is the screen.

What if:

. . . that is ALL you could play with: what is on that screen? You cannot look at past scenes or future scenes but only that which you can see. All of your amusement, information and engagement could only be from this screen, THE NOW SCREEN.

What if:

. . . the only opportunities that existed were available or accessible through this NOW SCREEN?

What if:

. . . you knew that you would never be bored, in lack, afraid or wanting because the NOW SCREEN could never disappoint? But you can't cheat either. You cannot let thoughts of lack or disappointment or anxiety or fear in unless they were presenting themselves on the NOW SCREEN. Then you would know exactly what to do.

Now, just plug in some good music from the Universal DJ known as "Shuffle" on your iphone or favorite music player for a soundtrack and see what shows up on your NOW SCREEN.

CHAPTER 25

COMMON QUESTIONS

Question:

How should one deal with negative emotions when trying to attract prosperity, love and joy?

Answer:

Most of us live in a state of trying to attract prosperity, love and joy. Who doesn't want these things? We all have negative emotions, they are habitual. Knowing that doesn't make it any easier.

We learn how to surf them. They are waves that just need to be navigated. To think that anyone is free from negativity is outlandish. Some people have just become so good at navigating their way through them, they don't experience much negativity.

When I am overcome with depression or self-doubt, I feel as if I am stuck. The first thing I do is try and realize that this storm will pass. Sometimes I feel like the storm is lasting forever and I am stuck in that place. It doesn't feel like it will pass, but the storm always opens up to clear skies eventually. But when?

- *Express* what is happening. This means I have to reach out. Whenever more than one gathers, spirit is there to help.
- *Take an inventory* of your vibrational diet. What are you eating, who are you seeing, how are you spending your time? What could you do to brighten all those things? We can stay in denial about our diets and actually think we are eating healthy when in reality we are not.
- *Reach out.* I reach out to someone who is nurturing, kind, loving, understanding, and evolved enough to just listen without feeling like they need to fix me.
- *Seek an expert.* Maybe my hormones are off, or I need acupuncture. Or I need some type of nutritional support that I am not getting. Sometimes I just feel dull and don't know what my upgrade needs to be.

- Most importantly, make sure you are having fun. Are you playing at all? Taking time off? Freeing up some mental real estate?
- Go to a movie that is emotional. Laugh, cry, experience emotions from an outside source. Take a break from your "isness" if your isness isn't happening.

Question:

How can we teach our children to have access to muse consciousness from an early age?

Answer:

Children are natural muses and live in the world of magic. Enter into their world with suspended disbelief.

- **Follow their examples!** When you enter into the magical domain of a child's world, why do we always have to be the wet blankets that say things like "Oh, that's only make believe." Or, in the "real world" that doesn't happen. Or the one I don't like the least, "When you grow up..." All of those remarks just discount the child's already perfect, mystical worlds full of natural play, fun and creativity.
- **Cultivate their created identities.** When a child is playing like he's Superman, make him

the cape. Call him Superman. Treat him like Superman. Assume he is Superman. This is teaching a child that the world of his imagination is safe and a feel-good place to be. This is also teaching a child that there are no limits and that everything is possible. We want children to know that this is a kind and joyful world and that we are here to enjoy and have fun.

- **Use the language of musing.** Rave about events that are magic and mysterious and wondrous.

- **Play in nature.** Expose them as much as possible to the natural world.

- **Set the example.** Children sponge up our belief systems by osmosis. Where do you stand on magic? Where do you stand on creativity and fun? How do you language these in your own life. How much does your child see you enjoying your passions?

- **Value desire.** As your child grows up and the conversations begin about what he or she will do with their life, speak in terms of what they love to do instead of what will make money or what career will be the most advantageous or prestigious or impressive. Let it be known that we direct our lives based on what we enjoy, which is usually what we are good at and are meant to do.

- **Speak to their divinity from an early age.** I remember when my daughter was six years old. One night while tucking her in she looked up at me and said "Who am I, I mean I know I am this (she touched her body) but who am I really?" After she said this I hugged her and told her how happy I was that she asked that question because it was such an important question and that is one of the reasons why we are here. My answer to her was:

> *"We are here to remember that we are God,*
> *and have fun while we are remembering."*

So how did my daughter turn out, now that she is 14 years old and was brought up to believe that she is God? I don't know yet, I'll have to get back to you on that one!

Question:

What are some red flags that send signals to us that we are off our true path?

Answer:
- Boredom
- Lifelessness
- Not enjoying our lives

- Time seems to slow down
- Feeling stuck

How can I get back on the path?

We get back on the path through enjoyment. Questions to ask yourself if any of the previous states are present:

What can I do that will totally sweep me away?

It could be anything like painting, dancing, walking in nature, playing bingo, digging in a sandbox, pirating roses, walking through a university, going to a book store and looking at magazines that appeal to you for no particular reason, lying on a blanket in the grass at a park anything that you get lost in.

What makes me giggle?

How can I escape what I am supposed to be doing and do something that I want to do for no reason? What are the simple pleasures I have forgotten, like going to get an ice cream at an old drug store, petting a dog or walking barefoot? Sometimes we forget what we love in the process of just trying to get through the day. When is the last time I read a good trash magazine and quit taking life so seriously? Why don't I just fake a smile today and see what happens?

How much music am I listening too?

If music turns you on... play all your favorites.

How can I get unstuck?

Try doing the opposite of everything you are doing. If you always take this route to work, try another one. If you always go to this coffee shop, try another one. If you always do a certain type of exercise, try a new one. If you always wear a certain look, be somebody different in your dress. Change everything in your routine. Shaking it up gets energy moving and before you know it, you are unstuck.

Question:

How can we discover what our true desires are if we have suffered emotional, psychological or physical traumas in our past?

Answer:

Who among us has not suffered from some form of trauma? We ALL have a story. The "story" is universal. It is the human condition. Otherwise, what have we been doing for the last 20, 30, 40, 50 years? Probably not living in bliss and deep satisfaction.

- See your story as just a story.
- See your story from a higher perspective. Did you know that some of the best healers, artists,

musicians and highly successful people come from abusive, tragic backgrounds? It is a pedigree to have an interesting story. Wear it well.

- Own your story and then let it go. One of the traumas of my life was the suicide of my boyfriend when I was 16 years old. It still has a charge whenever I bring it up. I am never in the mood to freely talk about it. When someone in my daughter's school had attempted a suicide, the whole tragic event got re-stimulated in me. But, it is just my story. It has helped make me who I am today. I will never be 100% free from the pain, it just is what it is. And in the end, it is just a story.

- Use your story. Talk about it, express it, seek therapy if that applies and then own it as part of the amazing circumstances that make you, YOU. Lance Armstrong used his trauma to launch an uber-successful career.

Question:

How can we overcome energy blocks in our creative or professional work?

Answer:

Shake up your routine. Go right now and play a song by Sly and the Family Stone or any other soul shaking song.

- Take some time for yourself
- Change your environment
- Do everything new, re-stimulate
- Walk through new doors
- Hire a muse
- Listen to music
- Play

Question:

What if I hate doing something, but I know I "need" to do it in order to get to my goal? For example, working out or studying for an exam, or making money at a job I don't like in order to build my career.

Answer:

Doing something you don't enjoy or isn't fun may be productive, but it's not sustainable in the long run, especially if it doesn't offer some sort of enjoyment or satisfaction. It can actually be counter-productive. But this is where it gets creative.

Welcome to the world of substitutes

If you are on a weight loss program, many times you will substitute. By this I mean find something that will still satisfy you. Instead of sugar you may use Stevia. Instead of bread, you may have flax crackers. You still scratch the itch; with a less negative impact.

Let's look at a few examples. You absolutely hate to work out but you need to get some exercise. You may hate to work-out but there is something you might like that doesn't FEEL like exercise to you. What about walking on a tree-lined path in New England in October? OK, maybe not realistic but you get the idea. It has to FEEL OK. What about a stroll in a park or a mall or roller-skating or operating heavy machinery? What about a water aerobics class, a tango class, archery or umpiring someone's soccer game? How about walking on a treadmill while reading your favorite gossip magazine followed by a heated sauna? Shopping? Strolling downtown at night to the yogurt shop?

But what about studying for an exam? You could find a public place to study and get a giant fancy coffee or take frequent breaks where you could people watch. Or treat yourself to small rewards every thirty minutes, like text flirting with your boyfriend. Something that makes it FEEL better than torture.

What about doing something like waiting in line at the social security office for 3 hours?

- Laugh. Well there is just no getting around some things. But you can laugh about the horribleness of it and be entertained by the hideousness of the experience. You can also bring a great book.

Question:

What about a job that you hate?

Answer:

As long as you are doing everything possible to find a job that feels better or a role that you are moving towards, then you are expanding. But at some point you are going to have to take a risk and jump. You do not want to be in the vibration of severe job dissatisfaction for long, if ever. We have to survive somehow and pay for our eating and sleeping habit.

The sooner you get out the better so that you can be in alignment with a job you like. The most important thing is to *find a substitute that feels good.*

Question:

What if I don't know what inspires me? What if nothing really inspires me? Is there something wrong with me?

Answer:

There is nothing wrong with you if you feel that nothing inspires you. It's just time to shake things up a bit. There are many reasons why we don't feel inspired. Depression, feeling trapped in a job we hate and seeing no end in sight to the misery. The common thread to all these reasons is the word "stuck." And that is just what we need to do, get unstuck.

The truth is, there is ALWAYS a desire. Even if it is a desire to become unstuck. That is a start. Focus on what you want, not what you are doing that you don't want, even if it is a new type of apple at the grocery store. Find a movie that you want to see. Want something and then move towards that.

Question:

How can I get out of my comfort zone without falling off the edge?

Answer:

Take baby steps. No one wants to fall off the edge or be thrown into fear and anxiety. When that happens all our energy goes to our second chakra of survival. Creativity and the lighter higher vibrations are hard to tune into when the Harley Davidson motor of the second chakra is overriding everything.

- Remember that great transformation can occur in small shifts.

- Sometimes we need to fall off the edge. I mean sometimes we just need to let our worlds crash. When we find that we are struggling to hold everything up and it is driving us crazy, it may be a time to just let go and fall down. Out of the ashes rises the Phoenix.

Question:

Why are there so many different "flavors" of consciousness for people to choose from? Why not just one?

Answer:

There is only one consciousness and that is wakefulness. When I refer to the Modern Muse as a new flavor of consciousness, I am referring to a new flavor of creative energy available to us all.

Summary

For all of the effort we put into ourselves to be happy, find our life purpose and achieve a sense of personal clarity or greatness, we must remember that inspiration is only the first step. Being a muse is about having the courage to be awake in a world that discourages embracing anything beyond what can be measured physically. To be your own muse is to allow inspiration to fuse all of the most important and mundane decisions of your life. The inner muse is about a new way of seeing how the spiritual and the physical worlds mingle and letting that intermingling serve as an inspiration to others on their own journeys.

You can have a ravishing life if you are led by the guidance, signals and non-physical cues that are as important as the floor you walk on, or the table you sit at. Muse consciousness urges a sense of being joyful, creative and playful as well as inviting magic back into your life. Remember that you ARE the muse of the universe, here to enjoy and spread your unique flavor of inspiration to others. That's it!

9031156R0

Made in the USA
Charleston, SC
05 August 2011